IN DEFENCE OF SHAME

IN DEFENCE OF SHAME

IN DEFENCE OF SHAME

Tanveer Ahmed

Connor Court Publishing

"A thoughtful and beautifully-researched exploration of shame, and the modern permutations of this ancient and uniquely human emotion.

"Fascinating. Ahmed brings clinical expertise and a journalist's curiosity to this eminently readable exploration of shame, and its surprising contemporary uses."

Annabel Crabb ABC broadcaster and author

"Fixing community is intertwined with mending ourselves. Blending vignettes from his patients with insights from social science, Tanveer Ahmed dives deep into the emotions of shame, anxiety and how they affect the ties that bind society together. A riveting read."

Andrew Leigh, ALP Shadow Finance Minister

"Tanveer Ahmed's writing brings together a remarkable breadth of cultural history grounded with concrete, real-life insights from his work as a psychiatrist. He is able to blend the abstract world of ideas with stories from the lives of people who are diverse on all measures: cultural background, gender, age, religion, and class. The result is a rich tapestry of insight into the contemporary human experience."

Claire Lehmann, Founding Editor *Quillette*

"This book succeeds in engaging with some of the most deeply entrenched problems facing society from a perspective that brings together the insights of psychology and cultural analysis. It provides a remarkably astute analysis of the relation between anxiety and shame and a compelling account of the real meaning of self-harm."

Frank Furedi, Professor of Sociology, University of Kent

Connor Court Publishing Pty Ltd

Copyright © Tanveer Ahmed 2020

PO Box 7257
Redland Bay QLD 4165
sales@connorcourt.com
www.connorcourt.com

ISBN: 9781925826876

Cover design by Josh Durham

Printed in Australia

This book is dedicated to my daughters, Katarina and Saskia, who, I hope, will continue to read books, even as their smartphones perpetually conspire against it.

ABOUT THE AUTHOR

Tanveer Ahmed is a psychiatrist and columnist for the *Australian Financial Review*. His past books are *The Exotic Rissole* and *Fragile Nation*. He lives in Sydney with his wife and two daughters.

CONTENTS

CONTENTS

"You can find shame in every house, burning in an ashtray, hanging framed upon a wall, covering a bed. But nobody notices it any more."

Salman Rushdie

INTRODUCTION

In my ancestral language of Bengali the word shame is called "Lajja". The immediate implication of the term is one of hiding. The term was made famous in a 1993 book, titled *Lajja*, by a Bangladeshi physician Taslima Nasrin. She wrote of atrocities by Muslim extremists against Hindus in Bengali villages, especially in relation to the demolition of the Babri mosque in India. There was a special focus on male violence and exclusion towards women. For her efforts she received a fatwa and multiple death threats. The book was banned, but later sold fifty thousand copies in the first six months alone. Nasrin fled the country and has lived in exile in Europe ever since. The book sold widely overseas and was translated into many languages.

I came across the title of her book while visiting Bangladesh as a medical student in the late 1990s, a few years after the book's publication. Nasrin had just fled the country and was a hot topic of discussion. Despite being born in Bangladesh, I had grown up in Australia since the age of six. I was careful not to wade into matters related to religion in a place like Bangladesh with very different sensitivities. But Nasrin's themes regarding what she believed was Islam's treatment of women were impossible to escape given part of my experience involved in visiting a shelter for victims of acid violence attacks.

I knew of such cases and had even met some victims during return visits to my parent's villages. But nothing prepared me for the collection of scarred, charred faces and stories of horrific abuse at the newly formed facility aimed at acid attack survivors. Some of the girls were barely teenagers. All were victims of wounded male honour, usually after rejecting advances, not producing adequate dowry or taking part in what were deemed to be inappropriate interactions with other men. The vast majority were from extremely poor backgrounds – children of beggars, maidservants or rickshaw drivers. Rarely was there someone from a middle class family, but they were usually desperate not to be identified. I was already familiar with honour killings, another example of extreme collectivism where a woman's actions were judged an insult to men and in turn the wider family's standing, but I had never seen such vivid examples of the cost of living amid a moral axis of shame and honour.

I was born in the city of Dhaka to well educated parents who were from poor, rural families. While I have little memory of it, we lived in a single room for my initial years before we migrated to Australia. Our dwelling was part of a large housing estate. I remember being ensconced in a collective from early in life, having a wide circle of friends and family always present, jostling for attention and resources.

A deeply traditional and religious society, there was no focus on building autonomy and independence in children. Attachment parenting was the norm. Physical punishment to regulate behaviour was expected. I endured many a beating without considering it unusual. Shame first became a notion in relation to the physical body, either to do with toilet training or clothing one's genitals. A typical shaming ritual was to be ordered to hold one's ear and perform multiple squats in front of a parent. I was amused recently when on BBC news I watched Indian police commanding locals in Delhi to perform the same ritual for not adequately socially distancing.

Interdependence was far more valued than independence. This was at odds with the values of outside society which encouraged individualism, autonomy and freedom. I was somewhat lucky in that my parents were not religious, allowing some flexibility with regards to socialising more freely. But it was always clear that we were part of an ethnic community where gossip was a potent weapon, enforcing conformity. There were narrow confines with regards to career choices and marital partners.

I used to look down on the deep traditionalism of my background, highlighted further by some of my experiences while visiting facilities such as the acid violence hospital. It stifled innovation, creative thinking and aspiration more generally. At its worst it trampled on individual choice so severely that it resulted in ostracism or even death.

Over time I have come to value the forces of tradition and a degree of collectivism as a force for good. Such forces were critical in maintaining some of the integrity of family and community that was being torn asunder in other corners of Western societies, especially among the poor. I grew up in a rough part of western Sydney so this steady unpeeling of the solidarity of working class life was already apparent. Fatherlessness, drug addiction, criminality and broken families were rampant among many friends and neighbours. This was usually in contrast with the tight knit nature of most ethnic families.

Growing up amid a traditional ethnic community in the West allows for an especially good combination of the best features of both cultures, an insight into the appropriate mix of independence and interdependence. The right dose of shame is an ingredient in such a delicate balance.

There are episodes in my childhood when I remember feeling shame and wanting to hide. One was being caught shoplifting at the age of thirteen. I was in a newsagent tempted by a set of gold lettered stickers. I eyed them as potential for a title page in my exercise books. I knew my parents would never buy such a frivolous piece of stationery. My relative incompetence in the act was immediately exposed by the shopkeeper who took me into a back room before calling my father. Expecting a thorough beating as I had already experienced on several occasions when having committed wrongdoing, I was instead subjected to an entire evening of silence. I saw from afar my parents sitting together at the dining table, eyes downcast, rolling balls of rice and dahl. An invisible cloud of abject disappointment lurked within the household.

This was especially magnified as I had just begun a full scholarship at one of the country's most prestigious private schools. Like many children of immigrants I was well on the path of fulfilling my parents' aspirations but that afternoon, dressed in a grey blazer down to my knees, I had hurt them immensely. I even heard my father talking about it to relatives in Bangladesh. I imagined a large audience encompassing my immediate and extended family all shaking their heads in unison. This was the epitome of shame.

The punishments I would endure at home, while rare, were at odds with what I experienced at school. There was a greater ease with Asian parents regarding the withholding of affection in response to academic underperformance or not adequately respecting elders or tradition. Meanwhile the worst possible punishment at high school was something called a "fatigue", a more active version of detention. I received two in my six years of secondary education, one for circulating a penis themed note in mathematics class and another for playing mock baseball using our leather bound diaries as a bat. The Latin teacher had left the room briefly, but just as she walked back, my rollicking shot of the squash ball ricocheted off a wall and on to her spectacle bound face. I was sentenced to an hour of repeated Latin conjugation – dominus, domine, dominum – after school. Perhaps it was equally effective in regulating behaviour given it was utter tedium.

Another episode where I felt a loss of individual dignity was crossing the border into Singapore while backpacking around the world, having deferred as a university student. It was rare that I felt my heritage from a country like Bangladesh, with its image of poverty and disaster, ever diminished me in Australia. Countries like Australia are probably the least racist in the world but are open enough to have the most heated discussions about racism. Yet I was held in custody for several hours while crossing from Malaysia into Singapore when the border guard was convinced my passport was forged. The key piece of information was my Bangladeshi birth. The guard was suspicious that I was more likely to be a migrant worker than an Australian citizen. I was in fact there to visit my uncle who was a migrant worker in a fax machine factory. I stayed with him briefly in a dormitory with five others, sharing a room sleeping in bunk beds.

I was unusually enraged by the experience of being held at the border, even though a supervisor stepped in eventually to wave me away mumbling a sheepish apology. I have since had another two experiences for similar reasons, once in the Middle East and another in Singapore. Both regions have large numbers of migrant workers. I have thought much over the years about why the experience enraged and affected me so much.

One reason was the clear underlining of how lowly many countries viewed my ancestry. I was made to feel incredibly small merely for my birthplace. This experience taught me the nature of humiliation and its difference to ordinary shame. While shame has potential usefulness as a signal to reorient people to a group's norms, humiliation has a different character of stripping someone of dignity. It is often a trigger to an ensuing rage in the humiliated, which was certainly the case for me as I shouted madly at the border police to no avail.

In the Middle East, for example, Bangladeshis were paid the lowest of any migrant worker group. Most arrivals were from poor villages with barely a high school education. I was incensed that I was being seen as part of this category. But in demanding that my Australian privilege be treated with more respect I felt guilty that I was confirming the bias against the migrant workers. The experience touched on something deeper, a reminder that there was a sense of shame and humiliation that came from my origins in poverty.

This is common for many immigrants and can be a deeper source of drive that elevates many to great success. While often unconscious, a sense of insecurity, and the associated fierce drive to rise up the social ladder, was an expectation held by most immigrants for their children. I know as a psychiatrist that the term narcissism is rooted in this experience of humiliation. This can potentially leave a hole that needs filling with constant affection and admiration, unlike the loose usage of the term today as a synonym for any kind of self-aggrandisement.

INTRODUCTION

One of the most renowned modern books about public shaming is by British gonzo journalist Jon Ronson who profiles several people who experience some version of public shaming. His book is titled *So You've Been Publicly Shamed* and is an exploration of modern versions of shame. While my interest is less about public internet shaming and more about the private permutations of this ancient, unspoken emotion, I did take a particular interest in Ronson's outline. The overlap of the public and private versions of shame was especially relevant at a time when social media blurred the boundaries. We were all both audience and performers.

One of the chapters featured Jonah Lehrer, a renowned American writer who wrote about psychological topics in books and magazines like the *New Yorker*. He was accused of fabricating a Bob Dylan quote and other instances of plagiarism. The downfall of his career was brutal. He has never been published in the mainstream press since 2012, a notable example of public shaming and associated career death in journalism.

I had my own experiences with associated plagiarism accusations, initially in 2012 and again in 2015. On both occasions I lost my columns at the *Sydney Morning Herald* and *The Australian* newspaper. It also meant I lost a chance to present a prime time documentary for the ABC which had just been commissioned, a gutting disappointment.

Lehrer's downfall occurred only months before my own and brought the issue of plagiarism in the age of the internet to special attention. This was a time of unlimited information sharing, the rise of amateur publishers like bloggers, all at a time when mainstream journalism was collapsing amidst the onslaught by tech giants upon the classified advertising market. Plagiarism was both easier to commit and expose.

My mistakes arose from putting together research via cut and paste throughout multiple word documents, but then not referencing them. I would put together my columns over several days in the evenings after completing my days as a newly qualified psychiatrist. The mistakes looked monumental when highlighted on national television. I had been rapidly promoted and was flushed with media opportunities. In the age of terrorism, there was a huge demand for Muslim voices. But my foundations in the trade were exposed as pretty shallow.

I knew it was wrong, but still did it. The career threatening nature of the mistake was not something I had been introduced to. It didn't really come up in a technical degree like medicine, unless you did research. I felt like I was just speeding a little, when in fact the journalistic police pulled me over to take away my licence. The emotion I experienced initially was a combination of embarrassment and shame. Embarrassment was more transient and less associated with selfhood. My fall was cushioned by many supporters. Among journalists the universal theme was along the lines of 'just don't do it again'.

In psychiatric circles, it was impossible not to compare my case with Dr Raj Persaud, a psychiatrist and BBC presenter, who lost his media roles a few years earlier due to allegations of plagiarism in his newspaper columns.

I became intrigued by figures like Lehrer and Persaud who had suffered a downfall. I knew nothing of them beforehand. I even had an email exchange where I expressed my admiration for Lehrer. I enjoyed the redemption of writers like British author Johann Hari, who returned from a scandal to write *New York Times* bestsellers, usually about mental health related topics such as drug addiction and depression.

I also noticed the over-representation of offenders of South Asian background. As well as Persaud there was the CNN host and *Newsweek* writer Fareed Zakaria who was a real superstar. He survived despite repeated cut and paste errors. Locally a promising young journalist Phil Jacob, the son of Indian financier and former Packer advisor Ashok Jacob, was exposed and fired from the *Daily Telegraph* in 2014. Months earlier Jacob was featured as one of *Cleo*'s most coveted bachelors.

It was difficult not to see some kind of cultural component, although I know this would be seen as making excuses. But in a book about shame and how the collective intermingles with individual experience, it is worth considering that sensitivities around plagiarism overlap with individualism, associated attitudes around intellectual property and what constitutes originality. It seems to be a pitfall in building media diversity. This may also be why in America, for the fiercest individuals, the opprobrium can be the strongest.

When it came to shame, I really felt it the second time in 2015. The error was relatively minor compared to the first, a few lines I didn't reference. But I didn't see it see it coming, evidence that I had incorporated a terrible practice as routine to some extent. It happened within months of my being given a new, major opportunity. The editor of *The Australian* at the time, Clive Mathieson, sent me a kind email telling me he knew it wasn't deliberate but, given my past, he had the reputation of the paper to protect. I was easy prey for twitter vigilantes who used software to highlight my errors after a column I wrote about domestic violence raised controversies. My chequered journalism record was now intertwined with the culture wars.

The second episode was only reported in journalistic forums, a kind of insider gossip. Friends outside of the media couldn't understand the big deal.

I completely understood the more serious meaning of plagiarism this time, given its implications of property theft. One journalist friend spoke of seeing the printers at the plant and the sacred nature of the words on the page as the newspapers rolled out. Plagiarism corrupted the sacred bond between readers and writers. This was the nature of a taboo, which was why journalists react fiercely to the charge.

The equivalent in psychiatry was probably a boundary violation, which was when inappropriate relationships were conducted with patients. I remember as a medical student vaguely recognising it was inappropriate. But it wasn't until I was more experienced that I had a clearer sense of what a massive breach of trust the action was. It threatened the sacred nature of the doctor-patient relationship that the profession depended upon. Taboos were a pointer to a practice that was existentially dangerous for a social or professional group.

The shame I felt had less to do with undertaking some kind of strategic fraud than letting key supporters down. Even my mother expressed her disappointment. Despite my errors being more negligence than malevolence, I had no excuses this time. I was livid with myself. Much like some childhood experiences, I had a similar feeling of an associated audience of family, colleagues and supporters shaking their heads in dismay.

But I was still a psychiatrist and by then had also been voted into local government. I regularly taught and lectured colleagues, students and trainees. I was hardly skulking around without a career. But I was someone who had a strong drive to write and was bumbling around in public trying to learn and apply the trade, one with its own culture and rules. Writing was still the most public expression of myself. I remained determined to get it right.

I've been lucky to still have supporters, even as the industry contracts and opportunities become scarce. They have usually been people with whom I had personal relationships who could make their own assessments about my character or senior executives who could see my career in the wider context of a changing media landscape.

The shame I felt was useful in that it provided me with a strong drive to improve. Major failures can impede or enhance motivation. For me it was the latter. It regulated my behaviour, although in medicine even serious errors would rarely play out in public and leave a google link for time immemorial. Public humiliation was basically the way the media regulated itself. Medicine had a stronger tradition and structure to allow for a reintegrative focus in any kind of shaming.

I lost countless opportunities, varying from speaking gigs to Board appointments to higher office, at a time when the first google page with your name was essentially your resume. I was even asked about it in the Prime Minister's office while being vetted as a prospective parliamentary candidate.

It was frustrating when there were so many other elements to my life. I had an unblemished career as a psychiatrist. I was involved in a host of community activities. I was a husband and loving father of daughters. But there was this perpetual Achilles heel from my writing life, shame's digital shadow, that kept staining any forays into the public realm. While outside of prestige journalism my actions were considered relatively minor, it was the world of prestige journalism that still regulated middle class reputations to a degree. There was always the tension whether my journalistic errors were something I did or perhaps a pointer to something I was.

I have often been asked by journalists about my experiences given I was a psychiatrist too. Perhaps I had a better ability to examine and tame my own failures.

While training as a psychiatrist, there was little or no discussion of the significance of shame in mental illlness, despite it being such a critical part of the culture in which I was raised. Part of the reason were the shifts in thinking within the psychological sciences.

The field can essentially be viewed as three different topics.

One was neuroscience which is brain chemistry. This was about our emotional chemistry and why medications could help moderate the most debilitating emotional disorders. This had gained great prestige in the decades leading up to end of the twentieth century when I had just completed my medical degree. It led to over-simplications of disorders like depression, which were often communicated as a "chemical imbalance".

I have a special interest in patients from ethnic backgrounds, especially as so many do not view their emotional distress through the language of mental health. Rising disorders like self harm and social anxiety have particular overlaps with shame.

The medicalised language that is on offer to process their experience is often inadequate. The moral or group-facing dimension, so critical to understanding the predicament of many patients, is sorely lacking. Likewise, in disorders like addiction, the over-medicalisation of the experience hampers many from recovery.

Another key category of my field was behaviourism, which was the idea that we had a set of thoughts that led to emotions. Our behaviour was also influenced by rewards and punishments. The growth and prestige of what psychologists do is rooted in this philosophy, that faulty thought patterns can be modified to help with problematic emotions like anxiety or depressed mood. The lay public often didn't differentiate between what psychiatrists and psychologists do, but the key difference was that a psychiatrist's training was grounded in human biology. It was also from this realm of behaviourism that movements like positive psychology became influential, positing a more sunny view of human nature. Such movements had an influence in sidelining remnants of our more primitive selves.

But psychiatry's history and prominence really grew out of what is known as psychoanalysis. This was made famous by Sigmund Freud early last century. The notion of psychoanalysis was that we were primitive, instinctual beings. Most emotional disorders were related to trying to regulate our primitive selves within the constraints and expectations set by the social world. Psychoanalysis was hugely influential in the first half of last century, influencing the culture and politics. The idea that we had an unconscious just beneath our awareness swirling with desire was a factor in unleashing many of the movements of the twentieth century. It was within this realm that shame was considered of great significance, but the field's influence had been steadily diluted.

Yet I have become more fascinated about the role of the primitive and irrational in human affairs. While my focus is on mental health, the place of shame has great implications for education and also the law. There are failures in these areas directly related to our relegation of its significance.

Despite our culture of stigmatising shame, its expression can often be an act of love, a signal that one is part of a human collective.

This book is an attempt to grapple with the misunderstood emotion. Shame is a proxy for our relationship to groups, morality and the primitive, and one that is re-emerging in unexpected ways in modern life.

CHAPTER ONE

Shame: A Potted History

A rkan's family thought he was possessed. A lanky character with glistening dark skin, his addiction developed as a result of him being attacked while working at a convenience store. Arkan developed a post-traumatic stress syndrome where he continued to wake in the middle of the night with visions of a man wearing a balaclava and brandishing a gun, demanding money. He had been exposed to drugs through some of his networks but his use had been casual, limited to a few times a year with friends. But his use skyrocketed as a balm to self-medicate his trauma.

Arkan was from a typically large Sudanese family with eight siblings. The parents had fled civil war and arrived in via refugee camps in Kenya. His mother brought cookies she had baked as gifts during our appointments. The family were distraught. They considered traditional healers, several of whom worked in their own "practices" in the suburbs of Sydney and Melbourne.

The family asked for advice about whether they should undertake a group traditional ceremony that included chants, dance and the consumption of herbal liquids. I encouraged it so long as he continued with the prescribed medications.

For almost a year, Arkan was hiding in shame, struggling to avoid relapse from his amphetamine use. Our treatment services had neither the language nor the resources to engage with this aspect of his experience. It was only when he felt purified ritualistically in the eyes of his extended family, and clan, that he was better able to engage in drug rehabilitation.

Arkan's example is a pointer to how traditional categories of mental illness can be limited in capturing the depth of the internal experience, especially when the vast majority of people see themselves less as individuals but as part of a collective. Despite having limited qualifications as a witch doctor, I also attempt to conduct rituals within the consulting room.

On one occasion Arkan's father, who had returned to Sudan having married again, was linked by a phone loudspeaker from a Sudanese town. The family sang a song together, something from Arkan's childhood, one challenged by civil war. The mother broke down in tears. Arkan expressed his sorrow for letting the clan down as well as a degree of anger towards his father for leaving the family.

I explained that there was a physiological dimension to Arkan's addiction. The drugs were a type of self-medication for the distress he felt from the petrol station attack, a balm to temper a psychological anguish. He may also have been more sensitised to such a reaction given his childhood exposure to mass killing and violence.

A fascinating shift occurred as the consultation progressed. Arkan steadily improved his eye contact, from initially keeping his eyes downcast, even while speaking to his father who was on the other side of the world. While it was true that there were cultural differences regarding eye contact, the gradual nature of the shift during the family meeting was striking.

As the dramatic encounter progressed, tears flowed and powerful emotions bubbled to the surface. The nature of shame as disapproval from a critical group was directly visible, as was a kind of healing from the wound embodied by him being able to physically face his loved ones.

The consulting room is one of the few places where it is acceptable to display an entirely negative set of emotions. One of its great values lies in this capacity for the patient to be openly unhappy, which has become very difficult in the context of modern society.

Shame is a subtle version of such a negative affect. The story of shame illustrates many of the trends in how we experience and communicate our internal state. Understanding it better is critical for us to form healthier human connections and experience better mental health.

We treat shame as a primitive emotion, a remnant of our animal selves. Shame lies in the origin story of Western mankind; the story of Adam and Eve in their naked, shameful selves is at the heart of the notion of sin. Like farts and burps, shame is consigned to be hidden, to be dealt with in privacy, alone. Jung called it the swampland of the soul.

Freud highlighted shame as being linked to our most primitive biological functions – sex and defecation: "through a long series of generations the genitals have become for us the pudenda, objects of shame, and even of disgust."

Shame at its most basic level can therefore be considered as a painful affect that is concerned with sexual matters and functions associated with bowels and bladder. These matters potentially evoke the contempt or disgust of others leading to us attempting to avoid their disapproval.

17

Shame thrives on the impulse to conceal and is compounded by the fact there is no discernible facial expression associated with it.

Unlike embarrassment, when flushed cheeks denote an exposed failing, or the droopy affect of sadness or the expanded sensory surface of the eyes when we're in a state of fear, there is no such physical signature for shame. Charles Darwin argued that emotions have an adaptive function, in that they offered some form of communication beneficial for ultimate survival. The emotions of horror and disgust look the same on the face of a Sydneysider as they do on a Nigerian, but not so for shame, despite its universality.

Along with guilt and humiliation, shame is regarded as one of the self-conscious emotions, but it is not always immediately recognised. These emotions are all associated with a negative evaluation of the self, although guilt may not always occur in the context of a group. Likewise, humiliation is one step more severe than shame; more strongly associated with a diminution of the self rather than with an inappropriate action.

Unlike fear, shame requires learning, something that tends to occur most often during childhood. Shame requires a cognitive capacity. The first stage of this education occurs during toilet training or the directions to cover one's genitals. There are some cultural differences in this regard, with poorer cultures and those nearer the equator favouring earlier methods.

Studies of parenting in East Asia have also illustrated how mothers are more willing to withdraw affection in response to a child's bad behaviour. Children in countries like Japan or Korea learn about the concept of shame early, at approximately two-and-a-half years of age.

Shame is making something of a comeback in Western societies, despite our historical attempts to banish it from both the public and private square. Scholar Gersten Kaufman wrote controversially in 1989 that "American society is a shame based culture, but shame remains hidden…there is a shame against shame". While Australia does not have the Puritan past of America, there are strong overlaps.

In a TED video seen by over ten million viewers, social researcher Brene Brown argued that shame was "a silent epidemic" and must be tackled head-on and remediated. She called it "the pre-eminent cause of emotional distress in our time". After her talk went viral, she received invitations to talk all over the world, but recounts how many organisations asked her to give a similar talk without mentioning shame or vulnerability. This is a pointer that negative emotions such as shame are not easily conveyed in a society that elevates cheerfulness and positivity.

Such negative emotions are more palatably expressed in medicalised, morally neutral terms like anxiety or irritability. This is a part of my interest in the primitive emotions like shame as well as the parallel importance of ritual.

I am often frustrated by the limited language many patients have in describing their experience, talking in medicalised terms like depression and anxiety. It is my job to always clarify by asking questions like, "What do you mean by anxiety or depression?", which might lead to a richer outline of their experience.

It is entirely the fault of my profession and a marker of its success in altering the way we communicate about our emotional distress. I have even had people I've assessed in jail tell me they're depressed after they've committed murder and been put away for years. This may sound humorous but it's a pointer to how we've become accustomed to talking about our emotions in medicalised terms without much consideration of the moral, spiritual or situational context.

Let's consider the historical element of shame to better understand the stigma now associated with it.

There are few cultures where shame has not existed as a way to regulate behaviour. Greek philosophers and Christian priests spoke at length about the best ways to utilise shame. The emotion is discussed extensively in the book of Genesis. Socrates used the term in reference to debate, intending to stir doubt and discomfort, whereby an interlocutor might be forced to admit that some pleasures must be restrained. Plato identified the emotion as a reaction to a gap between shared ideals and the behaviour of individuals. In classical literature there was not much of a distinction between guilt and shame.

Shame has a strong evolutionary usefulness in that it helps us codify appropriate behaviour. It has been a prototype emotion of millennia in human systems, outlining our biological roots as tribal or clan based animals. When you consider one of the great advantages that humans have is their ability to organise and communicate effectively in large groups, shame and its associated emotion of humiliation have played an important role.

Harvard professor and psychiatrist Judith Herman argues that shame is one of the primary regulators of "attachment, care giving, mating, social ranking, inclusion, exclusion and co-operation among primates". Herman expands that, while this may be the case in peacetime, fear and associated violence tend to take over during war when human societies are on the brink of chaos.

In the book *Shame: A History*, by historian Peter Stearns he writes that shame becomes more pronounced as humans organised away from hunter-gatherer communities into agricultural ones. There was a greater dimension of social regulation, especially with regards to sexuality. Agricultural communities focused more strongly on reproductive sex than hunter-gatherer ones.

From a variety of regions including ancient Egypt there were displays of adulterers to badly behaved students held in public stocks to allow the general public to walk past and express their disgust. Its use occurred across other realms, too, from punishment, defending honour, enforcing hierarchy, or as part of child rearing. Almost ten percent of Confucius's writings centred on shame.

Shame becomes more necessary as the nature of our groups became larger and require more sophisticated cooperation. The growth of language within groups also led to gossip, giving us further means to regulate people's reputations through shaming. While there were no tabloid magazines like *New Idea* or *OK* centuries ago, studies by anthropologists like Polly Wiesner, who focused on the Kung Bushmen of Botswana, discovered a tiny proportion of the conversation was praise. Over 90 per cent was criticism and ridicule. Similar proportions have been found in studies of modern societies, such as the conversations of university students in cafeterias.

Anthropologists have located a handful of cultures where the practice of shaming did not seem to exist. The San people in the Kalahari desert of Botswana and Angola were identified as a tribal group that used teasing and humour instead. The Malaysian hunting tribe called the Semai and the Utku Inuit group considered shaming unnecessary. Both groups valued shyness and were against physical displays or self-aggrandisement of any sort.

For the initial period of American colonisation, Western observers considered the limited use of shame among Native Americans a marker of their emotional inferiority.

Other cultures such as the Masai of Africa used it heavily, varying from a public, painful circumcision as a rite of passage for male adolescents to creation stories where Gods are shamed. One such deity blazes the sun after being injured by a goddess so that his injury would not be noticed.

One study compared an Indonesian fishing village where shame was the second most commonly mentioned emotion, as opposed to a contemporary Californian region where shame featured forty-ninth on a similar ranking scale. The villagers also gave reports of specific shamed stances such as a shrinking pose in public or shame-based suicides in the context of pregnancies out of wedlock.

As Stearns highlights, shame in such situations serves to motivate and display appeasement allowing for appropriate behaviour, but also arose among the Indonesians in competitive activities such as drumming, which was a central part of communal rituals. Young men felt shame because they were terrible drummers, a trait many households with struggling musician neighbours may be appreciative of today.

The villagers used the term "thick-eared" for people who did not exhibit the appropriate shame which rendered them suspicious. Many of the fears around shame overlap with being seen and less related to a moral compass. There is a greater emphasis on avoiding mistakes which can encourage conformity rather than exceptional performance.

There is also the important concept of anticipated shame. Because a key function of shame was to prevent unwanted activity, we anticipated the prospect of shame and in turn avoided the over-stepping of behavioural boundaries. This is known as "shamefast" and is regarded as the linguistic origin of modesty.

Sexuality was the key behaviour being regulated in Western shaming rituals. Some of the more notable examples include adulterers in classical Greece being called "donkey riders" as they were paraded around upon a donkey after being placed in public view. Other punishments for adultery including being dressed in a transparent tunic and displayed in the marketplace, the link between nudity and shame made explicit. In line with their innovativeness and originality in other worldly affairs, the Greeks even came up with the practice of "radishing" which involved male adulterers being held in stocks while a large vegetable was inserted into their anus, the reference to the female sexual role rubbing salt into the wounds of humiliation.

Versions of this parade for a shameful act were virtually ubiquitous across cultures throughout the Middle Ages. In Islamic societies there was a term called "tashir" to describe the practice. Public executions often followed for acts deemed especially heinous, such as treason. Public onlookers threw insults, spat or threw shoes, an image that may be recognisable to younger generations from the public shaming of the *Game of Thrones* character Cersei Lannister, dragged in chains across the cobbled streets, for her charges of treason. This kind of public shaming was a mark upon one's reputation, but the practice always hovered uncertainly between humiliation and possible redemption.

Versions of this shame are worth contrasting with other cultures, especially the Chinese. I remember during my early days of university when another medical student in my year, Kim, killed himself by jumping off the Gap, a well known cliffsite in the Eastern Suburbs of Sydney. He was of Korean background. A muscular, stocky young man, I played some casual basketball and Rugby with him. While I didn't know him well, he was familiar enough that I was deeply saddened and shocked by the incident. It later emerged that he was working in a butcher's shop to support his family as well as completing a medical degree. While we never quite know what goes on in the minds of suicide victims, the obligation and associated burden to his parents must have been immense.

I have thought of Kim many times over the years, especially considering South Korea lays claim to the highest youth suicide rates in the world. I am also reminded of him when I see patients from Asian backgrounds who present with psychiatric symptoms but are attending selective schools.

While selective schools often get a bad rap, they are worth considering because they give a pointer about differing ideas of shaming, and human nature in general. For the most part, Asian parents will view their children as resilient. There is little concept in the culture of self-esteem. Shaming practices will be more closely directed to academic achievement, which is also seen as a duty overlapping with familial obligation, often called "filial piety".

According to anthropologist David Jordan, shame in Chinese cultures "is the ability to take delight in the performance of one's duty." This has implications for some of our policies in education. In a multicultural society a focus on self-esteem and resilience may have a limited meaning for many children from non-Western cultures, although their experience navigating conflicting value systems can be a major factor driving emotional distress.

Shame has fewer links to sexuality in Chinese culture, unlike

Western history where the German word for shame, *scham*, is also a word for genitals. Shame in Chinese cultures has greater overlaps with not learning, being a servant or avoiding angry arguments if the person is well educated. This is a pointer to the importance of shame in regulating status hierarchies. Actors and prostitutes in China were required to wear a distinctive green scarf denoting their rank as the lowest social group. There are similarities with the strict hierarchies imposed within the Indian caste system, the "untouchables" being laden with negativity. There are also reports in Chinese culture of the notion of shame being applied to rulers losing territory, which may have implications for current geopolitical debates.

Some Chinese thinkers have also been eager to press how such a kind of shame is effective in internalising moral codes, stung by the view that guilt-based societies may be superior. Chinese are said to value shame over guilt because shame better guides real situations and relationships, rather than focusing on abstract standards. East Asians respond better to shame, seeing it as encouragement to self-scrutiny and improvements, rather than withdrawing like Westerners. East Asia is an example of a society where shame has been successfully combined with rapid economic and political development, including urbanisation.

The stigmatisation of shame began in the Western world with the great historical ruptures such as the French Revolution. Because these movements were tied with the conceptualisation of people as individuals, this diluted the importance of group ties. This is a pointer of how closely psychiatry, and in turn psychology, has originated from the Enlightenment, seeking to restore health by improving the reasoning responses of disordered individuals.

The historical project, the aim, was about trying to place order on a rational world, which required transformation of both the external and internal worlds of populations. It is no coincidence that Phillipe Pinel, the founder of French psychiatry, helped break the chains of the insane during the French Revolution and Benjamin Rush, founder of the American division of psychiatry, helped design the Declaration of Independence.

In contrast Sigmund Freud termed the project of the Enlightenment and the associated idea of progress a "benevolent delusion", a misguided attempt to deny the primitive, animal nature of Man. There has remained the tension between the population being characterised by the progressive ideal of the independent minded, non-partisan, well-intentioned and rational voter in contrast with the view that the masses are easily misled by false prophets, rumours and irrational passions.

Mental health has strong overlaps with the Western canon, which depends upon the belief in the individual and the significance of the internal, emotional realm. The moral axis of Christianity and associated Western social systems is often described as lying between sin and redemption. This suggests a strong internal component, whereas shame-based societies imply an external, group-facing dynamic. You are either honoured or shamed in response to clan or community.

It is not entirely clear how the process of steady diminution of the role of shame among Western societies in the past two-and-a-half centuries occurred. Scholars argue that Western societies had an especially punitive quality to the use of shaming, especially around sexuality, which led to a greater questioning of its usefulness. Urbanisation and greater diversity led to less tight knit communities. The Industrial Revolution and mass schooling also changed attitudes around child rearing.

Some philosophers have argued that guilt is a morally superior emotion because it focuses on an act and not an individual. By this reckoning, it also encourages the taking of responsibility, whereas shame can make us want to hide away. This is irrespective of whether there is a physical component to the shaming.

The rise of the Church and the State allowed for the outsourcing of physical punishments. Prisons helped make punishments a more private affair. Branding, public hangings and the pillory were removed within several decades of the turn of the nineteenth century across France, America and England.

This was in keeping with the view in legal circles that the State had a key role in preserving individual dignity. Shaming punishments ran counter to such an ideal. Several scholars argue that shaming has limited effectiveness in the urbanised, disconnected and largely anonymous societies of today: "Shame punishments are wrong because they represent an improper partnership between the State and the crowd," says legal academic Martha Nussbaum.

This is at odds with more conservative judges who view shame as an important tool in dispensing justice. Texan judge Ted Poe is one such character offering a revealing quote:

A little shame goes a long way. Some folks says everyone should have high self esteem, but that's not the real world. Sometimes people should feel bad.

Australian criminologist John Braithwaite is another believer that shaming has an important role in rehabilitating criminals. He brings together offenders with their victims as part of this belief, practices that have been trialled throughout the Western world under programs associated with restorative justice. As part of his research he visits countries like Bangladesh, Pakistan and

Afghanistan to better understand the place of shaming in the regulation of behaviour. Braithwaite believes good shaming is when it focuses on a deed and involves rituals of reintegration already incorporated within the shaming.

While shaming mostly occurs in a healthy context with such a reintegrative focus, philosophical movements decrying its use led to the growth of terms like "toxic shame" which was considered more dangerous; the kind that can lead to violence in susceptible individuals. As social worker Jonathan Fast writes:

> Shame that criticises what one is rather than what one does is considered toxic shame because it poisons self concept. What one does can be changed, but one is cannot.

When shame is used in a way to injure someone's self-concept, we can consider it more dangerous and even "weaponised". This is the category where behaviours such as bullying, harassment, bigotry and abuse lie.

When shame is poorly acknowledged and discussed in our culture, it is far more likely to be acted upon, just like other unacknowledged but powerful emotions. The physical body can take charge and express emotion if the mind is incapable or disallowed from doing so. This is why the notion of acting out is usually associated with children with poor verbal skills. But acting out is also associated with adults who are unable to identify or communicate difficult emotions. "Name it to tame it", is a well-known saying in therapy.

Journalist Jess Hill's lauded book about domestic violence, *See What You Made Me Do*, touches on this:

> Men who are shame-ridden can be like a tinderbox in

their relationship because...if they choose to replace that feeling of shame with a feeling of power, by attacking, they [can be] a very dangerous individual.

This greater focus on shame's damaging aspects to both the sufferer and any associated victims is a major factor in its negative connotation. It is also a pointer to its changing use within the politics of gender, previously disproportionately used in the context of female sexuality whereas now used in the context of male violence. This overlaps with progressivism's association of primitive emotions with traditional masculinity.

In their academic research about the difference between shame and guilt American psychologists Tangney and Dearing give the predominant view in our culture:

Our lives as individuals, as social beings, and as a society can be enhanced by transforming painful, problematic feelings of shame into more adaptive feelings of guilt. Recognizing the distinction between shame and guilt is an important first step in making ours a more moral society.

However guilt does not easily translate into many traditional cultures. For example, there isn't a word for it in many Asian languages. Guilt is barely mentioned in the Old Testament. Shakespeare used the term only thirty-three times, whereas "shame" is used over three hundred times. It can be argued that guilt is to a large extent a construct of the modern West.

This is relevant given we live at a time of declining religious belief, at least in Christianity, and raises the possibility that the notion of guilt may also be at risk. Guilt is dependent on a set of values having been internalised and overlaps with ideas of sin.

Guilt is an emotion that may have grown as we spent more time alone. Members of hunter-gatherer societies rarely spent time alone. In my early years I lived in the most densely populated country in the world, Bangladesh. On return visits, it is difficult to be alone for more than a few minutes. Inevitably, a relative, a servant or a phone call will intervene and ask about your whereabouts or current activity. Compared to such environments, in modern Australia almost a third of all households consist of just one person.

This historical context and the decline of shame in Western societies gives insight to recent history when anthropologists Margaret Mead and Ruth Benedict were among the first to classify societies according to what extent they were guilt- or shame-based. Benedict wrote about Japan and its use of shame to regulate morality in her book *The Chrysanthemum and the Sword*. There are few cultures more associated with honour and shame than Japan, home to the Kamikaze warrior and the practice of *seppuku*, ritual disembowelling in the face of being captured by the enemy in war. The action was aimed to restoring honour to the family.

The identification of shame to maintaining honour is most associated with the Japanese, although honour based killings in Islamic cultures is another notable example. In the code of the samurai it is said:

> Shame is the most important word in a samurai's vocabulary. Nothing is more shameful than not understanding shame. Crime belongs to the body but shame lies in the soul.

This is a pointer to what would be considered by many

Western observers as a pathological devotion to the cause of the identified group, which is the underlying driver of such acts. This identification can be real or imagined. In the case of the kamizaze bomber the psychological sciences call this altruistic suicide. A contemporary example is the suicide bomber associated with Islamic terrorism but perfected initially by the Tamil tigers in the Sri Lankan civil war. In the age of the internet, acts of extremism varying from Islamic terrorism or white nationalism are likely to involve individuals with psychological vulnerabilities who form attachments and belief systems through online interactions.

Social media has changed the boundaries of not just our public and private lives but also the historical trajectory towards the greater prioritisation of the individual. This contemporary dilution of the boundaries of the public and private has allowed for the re-emergence of a moral axis that was considered pre-modern and associated with more traditional societies.

Gossip through so-called "calling out" on social media can spread across the world in minutes. In his book, *So You've Been Publicly Shamed*, Jon Ronson recounts the story of Justine Sacco who, just before boarding a flight for work to Africa, lightheartedly tweeted that she was unlikely to get HIV because she was white. She arrived many hours later to discover that she had become an online pariah. Sacco says she continues to suffer to this day because her history is discoverable on any Google search. At least in terms of the world's digital memory, that tweet is what she will be remembered for. Sacco is a memorable but just one of many countless examples in today's era where careers and reputations have been trashed within days with few outlets for redemption or forgiveness.

There are situations when this kind of shaming may be rather

31

useful. Environment academic Dr Jennifer Jacquet writes about effective exposing of corporations in her book, *Is Shame Necessary?*:

> Digital technologies have at once lowered the cost of gossip and exposure and expanded gossip's speed and scope. This could make shame more salient to public life than ever before, especially since the power to use it has been put increasingly into the hands of citizens.

Jacquet argues that we need new rules for this historical era, and the effective use of shame is an important part of our overall armoury. This is especially true when applied to corporations or governments which are not capable of feeling guilt. She cites movements against fashion companies and their use of slave labour as a key success. Technology as a shaming apparatus allowed ordinary citizens to alter the behaviour of corporations into granting better conditions for low paid workers in developing countries.

However shaming also depends upon a shared morality which may be why it has had limited impact in financial circles where the criteria for success is firmly linked to profits, trumping any attempts to shame. The public hearings associated with the Hayne Commission on bank misbehaviour in Australia depended on linking the behaviour of bank executives to a morality recognised by the wider community. Fines or any reliance on guilt is deficient in such a situation.

Scholars of the internet, like Clay Shirky, put advances in communication into five categories: movable type, printing press, telegraph, recorded media, and broadcast and digital technologies such as the internet. At every stage of transformation in communication technology, the nature of shaming was modified and updated.

To understand how we might better apply shame usefully it is worth considering the same traditional societies when grappling with Christianity to offer insights into the relationship of guilt and shame.

In an essay for the publication *Christianity Today*, religious thinker Andy Crouch cites American-Chinese missionary Jackson Wu's dissertation "Saving God's Face: A Chinese Contextualisation of Salvation Through Honour And Shame". He highlights Wu's point that despite a contemporary understanding of Christianity through themes of sin and forgiveness, the stories of the Bible occur in societies that were steeped in honour and shame. Wu speaks to millions of Chinese Christians interpreting concepts of "face" through biblical stories.

Crouch developed his ideas after interacting with scholars based more thoroughly in Eastern contexts, such as China or Japan, to argue that our social media-stained modern life has partial similarities to the moral axes of traditional cultures. He ultimately describes the emerging axis as a postmodern fame and shame culture.

Fame is derived from the Latin word for reputation "fama". Crouch argues fame is a more public version of honour. A powerful currency of status, it is distributed by people with a very loose attachment to both the subject and to each other. While psychologists will argue that the lust for fame, so indicative of our times, is a desire to fill a gap in validation, it is arguably an appropriate response if we consider it a culturally suitable form of honour.

A key difference with the fame-shame dynamic is that there are no structured ways to prevent loss of face or rituals and processes to mend the risk of ruptured relationships. This is also why in cultures such as the Japanese there is a much greater sensitivity to direct conflict to minimise the risk associated with wholesale disagreement. The fame-shame culture has few strictures enforcing politeness or concern for "face" of others. The major crime is becoming excluded from the group norms, not a direct transgression of rights and wrongs.

An aspect to the healthy channelling of shame needs to be a greater focus on pathways to move away from an exclusively fame-shame dynamic. Better naming shame in its more sanitised forms is essential. This has the potential to limit the competition for honour and in turn the damaging, zero sum aspects of the worst features of shame.

The historical trajectory of shame is important in considering its metamorphoses into more medicalised, secular terminology. The emotion lingers in the corners of the mind, often unable to be named or identified, corrupting our relationship to the groups within which we might congregate. Let us now consider shame's relationship with the most common expression of emotional distress in our society.

CHAPTER TWO

When Anxiety Is Shame

Anxiety is the idiom of our times.

It is heartbreaking seeing patients visibly shake, hyperventilate or even hold back vomiting during interviews. This can happen as they describe their fears, recall traumatic incidents like car accidents or get teary about merely facing other people.

Despite us living, at least pre-coronavirus, in the most prosperous and peaceful time in history, anxiety disorders have never been higher. While this is partly due to measurement, there can be little question that we have a collective risk management failure, given anxiety disorders are an overestimation of personal risk in our daily lives.

The relationship between shame and anxiety is a good analogy for how discussion about mental health has evolved. Shame is a word with strong moral and social connotations. Our mental image is of someone with their head bowed, perhaps hidden from view.

The emotion of shame is also a pointer to a more primitive, darker side of our nature, the parts our upbringing had a duty to civilise. There is an implicit connotation that people are automatically connected to some kind of group; that we can't be conceived of as individuals alone.

In contrast, the term anxiety sounds medical. It has no moral attachments and evokes a private terror, the suffering of a lone individual. There is a strong physical dimension to the term, which is appropriate given that the experience often includes the heart beating faster, hyperventilating, or stomach cramps. Any kind of community is not invoked except in the subtypes of anxiety, such as social anxiety.

Anxiety didn't even exist as its own category a century ago. Freud categorised the term as either angst when it involved a specific fear, known as an object, and a neurotic anxiety when the fear was generalised. He did mention shame and viewed it closely linked with guilt and anxiety. Freud described shame as intertwined with condemning thoughts, a sense of imminent harm and a feeling of being exposed.

Anxiety has been seen variously as a medical condition, an intellectual problem by Enlightenment philosophers, a spiritual condition, and a stress response among people living in Anglo-Saxon societies. One thing all anxious people have in common is a pathological tendency to focus inwards.

One of the first major books with the title of anxiety was published in 1950, *The Meaning of Anxiety*, by psychoanalyst Rollo May. The diagnosis of social anxiety was categorised only in 1980, another example of how discussions around anxiety are relatively modern.

The lack of a clear definition of anxiety is perhaps the reason why it has become a blanket category to describe all types of emotion, including shame, many of which have more complex meanings.

The genetics of the condition received a boost in 2002 when the popularly termed "Woody Allen gene" was identified by Harvard University. The gene appeared to activate the part of the brain called the amygdala. The amygdala mediates our fear responses, a reptilian throwback that scans the environment for threats. While the term anxiety may not have been used, discussions about faulty cognitions were centuries old, presaging modern-day cognitive behavioural therapy that psychologists perform to modify catastrophic thought patterns.

American author Scott Stassel writes in the personal examination of his own challenges, *My Age of Anxiety*, which he intermingles with historical analysis:

> Anxiety is a function of both biology and philosophy, body and mind, instinct and reason, personality and culture. Even as anxiety is experienced at a spiritual and psychologist level, it is scientifically measurable at the molecular and physiological level. It is produced by nature and by nurture. It's both a hardware problem (I'm wired badly) and a software problem (I run faulty logic programs that make me think anxious thoughts).

While there is a universality to anxiety, the condition tends to present differently according to culture. Panic attacks are a more likely descriptor in Australia, whereas fainting is more common in Japan. Many of my Bangladeshi patients will cup their forehead to describe headaches and dizziness but are referred to me after their family doctor can't find anything physical to explain the problem.

Studies suggest that antidepressants do not always work as well in the Chinese. There is a condition known as kayak angst, described within the Inuit tribes of northern Canada. This affliction manifests in men who become scared to go seal hunting, which in our society would be called agoraphobia, experienced by people who feel overwhelmed in large open spaces or crowds. A common question I ask when I assess this potential vulnerability is what my patients are like in shopping centres or on public transport.

The *Diagnostic and Statistical Manual,* which lists the various classifications of mental disorders, divides social anxiety into that which involves public performance as opposed to the act of some kind of social interaction. The two often co-exist. Some of the world's most significant figures suffered performance anxiety. Jerry Seinfeld jokes that public speaking rated as the single biggest fear in surveys of the American population, one spot higher than death. This suggests, he says, that most people would rather be in the coffin at a funeral, than give the eulogy.

Part of my interest in writing about shame and its overlaps with anxiety is the sheer number of patients who are terrified of being scrutinised by other people, because of the chance they will be negatively evaluated. What they really fear is the potential for social humiliation, which many people experience as no different from a life-threatening encounter. Their fear is not without basis. Brain scans have shown the pain of social rejection is felt most intensely during adolescence. The experience is neuro-chemically indistinguishable from excruciating physical pain.

This is one of the most common causes of morbidity in an otherwise physically healthy and prosperous population. By morbidity I mean problems that aren't going to kill you but impose significant limitations on your quality of life. There are countless numbers of people who spend their lives trying to avoid other people. This fear paralyses their ability to conduct relationships or manage meaningful work, especially in a service economy where interpersonal interactions are essential.

The requirement for social performance in work or social settings is considerable but is also less structured than in the past, which probably compounds the anxiety experienced by people. Psychoanalyst Erich Fromm said this aspect of modern life meant we all required "a marketing orientation", which is perhaps a technical way to say self-promotion.

The steady inability to form meaningful connections is then the key contributor to bouts of depression and substance abuse. Many of the people I am asked to assess in prisons give histories where they have always been socially anxious and drugs were a way to help them interact.

The blushing associated with embarrassment is worth considering as an experience somewhere in between shame and anxiety. The first account of a fear of blushing was published by a German physician who described a medical student driven to suicide. Charles Darwin also wrote about the act of blushing: "It is not a simple act of reflecting on our own appearance but thinking of others thinking of us which excites a blush".

Shame overlaps with both blushing and anxiety. Blushing is a physiological indicator of our self-consciousness and our social selves, a manifestation of both self-awareness and sensitivity to how others perceive us.

Evolutionary biologists interpret blushing as a signal to others that we are deferring to someone of higher social rank, that we are feeling modest and self-conscious.

French physician Hartenberg wrote about social anxiety over a century ago, calling it "timide" and recognising it as closely linked to feeling ashamed. The founder of cognitively behavioural therapy, Aaron Beck, also argued that treating social anxiety was about minimising our fear of disapproval and inoculating ourselves against shame. This is partly what exposure therapies aim to do for those who are trying to overcome past traumas. Placing someone with arachnophobia among spiders may seem cruel, but a gentle grading of contact, from pictures to close contact, is the path to the cure.

There have been controversies around the diagnosis of social anxiety, with some of my colleagues criticising it as primarily an "Asian disorder" linked to shame-based societies. This is another pointer to how shame has been stigmatised in Western cultures, a form of Orientalism, prompting novelist Salman Rushdie to write, "Dear Reader, shame is not the exclusive property of the East". At a time of meritocracy, when there is an explicit pressure to achieve and rise up the social ladder, there is a moral component attached to social mobility.

In Japan the outward promotion of shame is encouraged and socially acceptable. For example, the avoidance of eye contact, displays of deference, and experience of shame are norms of the culture.

American psychiatrist, Michael Liebowitz, from Columbia University, wrote a research article titled, "Social Anxiety: The Neglected Disorder", in which he argued there was massive un-der-diagnosis of the disorder. The drug company Glaxo Smith Kline embraced the article and launched the medication Paxil – called Aropax in Australia – specifically for the social anxiety diagnosis.

"Imagine you were allergic to people", was the headline for one of the Paxil advertisements in the US. These kinds of promotions have also led to controversy surrounding the medicalisation of ordinary human behaviours such as shyness. My retort is that the demands surrounding extroversion in combination with the greater isolation of modern life mean what in other times may have been less debilitating require intervention today.

Sydney is one of the world's most multicultural cities. There are many newly arrived immigrants from the developing world who are ensconced in the dynamic of traditional cultures despite living in a modern, urban metropolis. I grew up to a large degree in such a dynamic with a focus on family *shomaan*, which is the Bengali word for honour. The power of shame is even more pronounced when the traditional focus on honour is married with the strict behavioural regulation of Islam.

This is most pronounced in the communities where relatively unskilled communities form ethnic enclaves, which can limit the interactions people of say Arab or South Asian groups have with other ethnic groups. These also tend to be the groups in which practices such as arranged marriage, attendance at Islamic schools and satellite television are more common. Whereas in the past some migrants returned to their native countries because they were struggling economically or felt too detached from their original culture, the incentives to do so are less pronounced given the power of modern communications technologies to mitigate any sense of disconnection.

Those patients who have grown up in Arab cultures, such as the Lebanese community, are often most ingrained into shame/honour cultures despite having lived in Australia for many decades. Group norms are intensely policed through gossip, humiliation and exclusion. They are also the people most sensitive to what many of us might experience as fairly trivial acts, such as not being appropriately acknowledged. Those from strict honour cultures may feel provoked by acts they consider as disrespectful, hence the word "dissed" that arose as an abbreviation.

A good example illustrating some of these tensions is a patient of mine, Hakim, who worked as a teacher at a major Islamic school. In his late twenties and devoted to his work, one evening he was walking through the inner city after visiting a nightclub and consuming a small amount of the party drug ecstasy. He was caught by police for drug possession with his gay lover, a relationship that was highly taboo in both their communities. His partner was of Iraqi descent and also a working professional. Hakim came to me for a psychiatric report to be presented at court, outlining his history of an anxiety disorder and past episodes of depression.

Hakim had an identity as a homosexual that was completely unacceptable to his immediate family and also the school community which employed him. That there may have been Australian laws preventing his discrimination did not matter. It would have been impossible for him to work at the high school if the parents became aware he was gay. In Arab cultures, homosexual acts are something people do, but not indicative of a homosexual identity. The public proclamation of such an identity, whether expressed voluntarily or by force, is unacceptable and brings dishonour to the family. I have tried on several occasions with devout Islamic families to help them understand that being gay is not a crime, but this does not usually progress as the community opprobrium is too great. The same sex marriage vote was notable for the low number of yes votes among Islamic communities living in Sydney's western suburbs, a marker of the great stigma attached.

Hakim had experienced prior bouts of anxiety. In our society, anxiety is one of the most acceptable ways to communicate emotional distress. Anxiety has a greater overlap with thinking.

The psychological treatment is usually cognitive behaviour therapy, which aims to modify thinking and in turn alter the negative emotions that might be attached to negative thoughts. But primitive emotions such as shame or humiliation do not fit neatly into traditional models of therapy.

The challenge, in attempting to treat Hakim, was that his problems were related to how his behaviour was enforced by the group with which he was closely associated. Psychological therapy is focused on internal states and has limited powers to influence group behaviours. Family therapy could help with the dynamics of small families, especially problematic communication patterns, but social norms and practices are outside the power of individual therapies.

So it was no surprise that in my psychiatric report I could offer only a formal diagnosis of anxiety. This was how Hakim's symptoms fitted into the acceptable, modern categories of psychiatric terminology. But underlying his anxiety was deep shame and the fear of being ostracised by his clan and family. There was also a genuine desire not to hurt his loved ones, who may have been subject to their own opprobrium by the wider community, especially when they fronted communal rituals at the mosque or at weddings.

These were the sessions where I felt the most helpless, when the source of the distress lay in cultures of shame and honour, in group dynamics. The audience that was in the mind of Hakim was never in the consulting room physically, but was critical to his recovery. Nor did I have any power to engage that wider group. Unlike my Sudanese patient Arkan, I was not in a position to involve the family or clan in any treatment. There would be no rituals by a witch doctor with a special interest in homosexuality.

Hakim would be mortified if I attempted to engage the family given the illicit nature of his activities.

I was at least able to help my patients understand the source of their distress. They were better equipped to integrate their sense of shame into a more coherent identity with less self-loathing. The occasional antidepressant also helped reduce their physical levels of anxiety but the root cause could not be modified.

I was able to get Hakim off the charges without a record or notification to the school. Instead, the magistrate directed Hakim to follow my treatment plan. But he will continue to keep his sexual identity as hidden as possible, and even consider marriage to a woman in the future to appease his family.

There is no online component to Hakim's sense of shame. There are much stronger group ties than the looser ones built online. But the shame enforced online can feel more permanent as it exists on record, unable to be erased, with merely the potential it will become less prioritised by search engines. There are few formal rituals or practices that help the modern forms of shame to be purified, but the corollary is that online group ties are relatively weak. The victim can usually move on to form ties with other communities.

One of the theories about depression and anxiety, especially among those with an evolutionary biology bent, is that they are signals about our status within hierarchies and groups. Socially anxious individuals tend to over-utilise the social rank system and under-utilise the affiliation system.

A key aspect of the rise in social anxiety is the greater form of status anxiety, notably written about by acclaimed pop philosopher Alain De Boitton in a book with the same title, *Status Anxiety*.

Meritocracy has both freed us to imagine infinite possibility but also opened up the distinct possibility that our position in the world is the cause of our actions and outlook. In such a situation, fear lies at the root of envy, a close relative of anxiety and shame; "the fear of not having what one desperately needs to have", according to British psychoanalyst Adam Phillips. There is a moral dimension attached to social mobility. As a result one of the most acute, modern versions of shame is social anxiety, the feeling attached less to a failure to do one's duty, as shame has historically been, to one of feeling unlovable.

Socially anxious individuals are attuned to cues and signs of dominance and to the competitive dynamic of the social world, frequently at the expense to signals of affiliation. This is significant at a time in history when people's affiliations are at an all-time low. Perhaps this description of individual sufferers is a wider pointer to the ills of modern society.

The socially anxious evaluate themselves negatively. As a result, they avoid undertaking actions that might be seen as bidding for status or approval, instead associating these claims with conflict, disgrace or rejection. Such claims can also be seen as showing vulnerability, essential to signal a desire for association.

The hordes of the modern shy can struggle in shifting from small talk about the weather or traffic to trivial discussion that might invite scrutiny. The fear of competition is associated with potential conflict. But there is still a need to remain in the social arena, which leads such people to recruit submissive behaviours both in a verbal and non-verbal form. Avoidance is one of the most common submissive behaviours.

There may be a period of adjustment that corresponds to an episode of depression. But we then adjust to our new position, whether real or perceived, and get on with our lives. This gives us an insight that much of what we call mental illness today, especially among those on the anxiety or depressed spectrum, involve people who have an acute sensitivity to social status in interpersonal interactions, in particular with regard to expressions that might be construed as negative. The chemical serotonin, which is linked to theories of depression, is associated with our position in social hierarchies. Alpha males in chimps have been shown to have higher levels and vice versa when we lose social rank. When we add the online world, much of our responses relate to imagined or virtual groups.

Many such reactions occur unconsciously to stimuli that the anxious are unaware of, something proven by MRI studies. Such finely tuned social perception may have conferred adaptive advantages but it's possible such stimuli in a media-rich environment geared towards social comparison contribute to perverse, unhelpful reactions. Whether we know it or not, we keep getting signals that make us doubt our relative social position, even as we traverse our routine, workaday lives.

There is rarely a patient I see who does not have some component of anxiety. Parents bring in their children worried about the diagnosis of ADHD, but nine times out of ten, the child suffered separation anxiety when starting school, became overwhelmed under pressure from a young age, experienced panic attacks in the midst of social scrutiny or struggled to apply themselves in assignments.

But the very experience of anxiety requires a degree of what is known as psychological mindedness, an ability to name the emotions. Most people experience a surface aspect of a bigger engine of their psyche. Much like oceanography, most of the iceberg of our psyche is below the surface. An aim of psychological therapy is to help shift up the invisible bits of the iceberg. This can also be quite upsetting as our minds often shift what is most painful away from awareness.

The consulting room is a modern version of confession, where patients discuss their secular sins categorised as symptoms. The greater medicalisation of the human experience has allowed for more people to comfortably seek help but also limited the language to describe our experiences. College studies in America have concluded that the current generation can barely discuss moral problems presented to them because they have become so distant from the language. We tend to be morally inarticulate. Half a century ago most of our various traits and behaviours might have been referred to as our characters, a term which immediately carries a moral connotation. In contrast today we are more likely to be referred to in terms of our personality, a term which is stripped of any moral meaning.

Some of the world's most renowned psychologists have argued that banishing the moral component of emotion has gone too far. Martin Seligman, the founder of positive psychology, asserts that social science had long turned its back on "Victorian moralising" and instead emphasised "egalitarianism" by promoting environmental causation rather than character. Seligman goes on to write:

> In this age of postmodernism and ethical relativism, it has become commonplace to assume that virtues were merely a matter of social convention...the time has come to resurrect character as a central concept to the scientific study of behaviour.

Australia is second only to Iceland in our per capita use of antidepressants. Those who criticise psychiatrists as dishing out too many medications will be surprised to find that we spend a great deal of our time explaining to people why our medications won't solve all their problems. Our culture appears to have a great deal of stigma attached to allowing spaces to think about the point of our lives or deal with difficult emotions.

But the rise of medication to treat our inner demons coincides with some powerful cultural currents. For the past half-century there has been a greater focus on life's purpose as self-fulfilment. The countercultural currents of the 1960s unleashed a wave of disruptive energy, coinciding with the emancipation of women and minority groups.

The greater focus on self-fulfilment had a dramatic impact on the psychological sciences, with movements away from merely treating the unwell. This trend was in keeping with Freud's comments that the profession's role was not to make people happy but to turn the sheer agony of severe psychiatric problems into "common unhappiness". But common unhappiness was too low a bar for such a demanding generation coming of age in the second half of the twentieth century, a time when the possibilities in life and work seemed stratospheric.

The improvements in psychopharmacology dovetailed with the emerging fields of positive psychology and happiness studies, the subject of the next chapter. The fall of the Berlin Wall and the discredited nature of communism also diminished the prestige of social policy, encouraging personal transformation instead.

The historian David Herzberg wrote about the new growth of psychiatric medications as offering a potential panacea for human potential and allowing "control of the brain so precise that it would permit doctors beyond curing illness to providing a nearly unlimited range of consumer choices for custom built selves". Antidepressants promised to "enhance, augment, and otherwise improve normal and emotional states as desired".

Colleague and author of the blockbuster book *Listening to Prozac*, Peter Kramer coined the term "cosmetic psychopharmacology". He argued for a kind of pharmaco-utopia, where the new suite of psychotropic treatment "could change people in ways they want to be changed – not just away from illness but toward some desirable psychological state". Despite being criticised for potentially encouraging a brave new world of chemically enhanced humans, Kramer also warned about whether "we are using medication in the service of conformity to societal values", namely productivity. This is especially relevant in diagnoses of ADHD and anxiety disorders among high socio-economic groups.

But for the discussion on the growth of social anxiety, its relationship to shame and the changing nature of group connections in our high-tech society, Kramer presaged a wider insight about what the huge success of psychotropic drugs said about our current stage of history: "The success of Prozac says that today's high tech capitalism values a very different temperament characterised by confidence, flexibility, quickness and energy".

Much has been written about how we live at a time when there is a great distrust of moral authority and of traditional institutions. There is suspicion about any system of values, given we have passed through the world wars, the demise of communism, the financial crisis and a rapid decline in traditional religion. Free-floating fear, which is technically called generalised anxiety, is heightened as we lose a cherished set of values. In his book *Culture of Fear*, social scientist Frank Furedi writes that primacy of fear in our lives links to this "motivational crisis that stems from the feeble status of moral authority".

The daily struggle of people living in prosperous Western countries like Australia is usually a tale of the individual trying to make his way in and against the demands of society. This struggle may vary from trying to maintain healthy relationships to forging an identity and participating in the battles for status and recognition. Within this tension is where people communicate and apply their values. This has, for large portions of the population, supplanted the twentieth century fulcrum of politics being between labour and capital.

There has also been a historical tension between periods of introspection that the early twentieth century aroused, and in those cultures where the notion of a private, personal realm did not exist. Earlier societies were predicated on an ascribed identity within a hierarchy and clan. The locus of the world existed externally and in relation to groups.

Is it possible we are re-entering such a time, as depicted by author Pankaj Mishra in *The Age of Anger*, where "Enlightenment humanism and rationalism cannot explain the world we're in"?

If there was an unleashing of desire last century in terms of consumerism and sexuality, modern distress is less likely to be privatised than to be politicised into unpredictable, disruptive movements. From vegan protests to Extinction Rebellion to the rise of white nationalism, ideology is far from dead.

Every week I see a patient who expresses an interest in UFOs or past lives, or has an obsession with Star Wars or animal liberation, an indication there is no less pining for value systems. The urge is merely taking on new forms and infecting our politics. Psychologist

Clay Rutledge writes in his book *Supernatural: Death, Meaning and the Invisible World* that belief in phenomena that exist beyond the physical world is an ingrained human impulse, that we are primarily meaning-seeking creatures. Supernatural forces like ghosts, gods or aliens help give a sense that there is a higher power overseeing our lives.

There is more religious zeal in politics than ever before, especially when fewer people have some kind of alternative source, such as Christianity, to gain their ultimate sense of purpose. When patients walk in for the first time to discuss their symptoms, it may be one of the rare times when they've actually had to ponder the point of their existence. We have so many distractions in modern life, from long hours at work to the unending novelty of screens to a buffet of leisure opportunities.

So many of the anxieties expressed in the consulting room are a pointer to the collective anxieties in the public realm. The power invested in my profession has grown as people have become sceptical or demoralised by the prospect of politics or participatory democracy being able to make a difference in their lives.

If schizophrenia was the appropriate mental illness befitting the Cold War, with the undercurrent of paranoia, the swings and lows of the 1980s capitalism befitted a diagnosis of bipolar disorder. The values morass of the current day appears to best favour a lost, heightened anxiety. It is difficult to see history as having been stalled, living as we are through Trump, the tumultuous events of Brexit, the rise of a whole new kind of politics throughout Europe and the ever-present inevitability of China becoming dominant, diluting American exceptionalism. All of this has been further complicated, or perhaps sped up, by the coronavirus pandemic.

The focus of the therapy shifted postwar to one of identity, in keeping with the forces unleashed from the 1960s onwards of the counterculture and individual fulfilment. Most patients in the private sector present with some version of anxiety or generalised phobia, or alternatively a malaise about the pointlessness of their lives.

The Harvard psychology academic Stephen Pinker writes most passionately about our current times being the most peaceful and prosperous in human history. We are much less likely to experience a violent death or die of a sudden, infectious disease. This is part of a wider trajectory of reduced violence and disease as we moved from hunter-gather societies to state-based, urban ones. Yet we have the highest rates of anxiety disorders in human history. While measurement and reduced stigma may be factors, the growth in the discussion of mental health indicates some exceptional qualities of the current moment.

We are collectively suffering from a risk-management failure, in the words of business strategists. Anthropologist and author Jared Diamond touches on this when comparing risks for native tribes in comparison with Westerners:

> Traditional New Guineans have to think clearly about dangers because they have no doctors, police officers or 911 dispatchers to bail them out. In contrast, Americans' thinking about dangers is confused. We obsess about the wrong things, and we fail to watch for real dangers.

We go through life calculating heightened risks, varying from terrorism attacks to social rejection, all of which limit our capacity. Some might say that in our current period of economic uncertainty and social disruption, anxiety may be an adaptive normality.

But I contend the term anxiety is losing utility just as it becomes too widespread. It delegitimises the original origins of the term, which, much like shame, had connotations of group identity. By reducing the experience to an individual, we encourage isolation. The lack of any moral or metaphysical connotation also limits people's understanding of their wider experience. The bland, secular overtones of the term contribute to a limited capacity for personal improvement and help to stigmatise any negative emotion. While it is social anxiety that is most closely related to shame, I want to examine how a culture allergic to negative emotions overlaps with other aspects of mental health.

CHAPTER THREE

Self-Harm and the Tyranny
of the Positive

Self-harm is one of the most challenging aspects of working in mental health. Every day I see patients with cuts on their forearms, sometimes partially covered with long-sleeved tops, other times voluntarily exhibited. Others burn themselves with cigarettes, bang their heads against walls or scratch themselves till they bleed. Taking overdoses of tablets is a common way such patients end up in hospital. The vast majority of them do not want to kill themselves. Unfortunately some do, especially if the act is combined with alcohol and drugs. Many celebrity deaths have occurred after such concoctions, à la Heath Ledger.

Despite living in a time when mental health concerns are more visible, there is no clear consensus on whether certain conditions are on the increase. There are many variables contributing, not least in terms of measurement and definitions of terms. But self-harm is one such affliction we can be fairly certain has increased.

This is confirmed in the studies, suggesting a tripling of incidence over the past two decades. There are similar trends in Britain, according to the UK Children's Institute. In America, a recent study in *The Journal of Pediatrics* found a 268 per cent increase in self-poisoning among children aged between ten and twelve in the years 2010 to 2017.

It is no surprise then that psychiatry's much cited handbook the DSM, or *Diagnostic and Statistical Manual for Mental Disorders*, often called the bible of psychiatry, finally included self-harm as one of its official categories in 2013. It came under the title of "non-suicidal self-injury". The British social historian Sarah Chaney, in her book *Psyche on the Skin*, heralds this as a breakthrough in the history of self-harm, which much like shame, tends to be covered up both physically and metaphorically.

Chaney outlines some of the history, from self-flagellation by the eleventh century Benedictine monk Pater Damian, who said, "When I freely scourge myself with my own hands in the sight of God I demonstrate the same genuine and devout desire as if the executioner were here in all his fury".

Chaney also outlines John Marten's 1712 pamphlet, "Onania: or the Heinous Sin of Self-Pollution", which suggests masturbation was seen as a loss of self-control close to self-injury. She touches on the ritual castration practices of the Skoptsy, a fringe sect of the Russian Orthodox Church, a notable detour into the past expressions of self-harm. A century ago, in the heyday of psychoanalysis, self-harm was seen as an illustration of the "death instinct".

Self-harm has always occurred in a cultural and historical context. Given we are currently living at a time when self-harm appears to be on the increase, examining the social context is essential.

I have several patients who are involved in self-harm groups. They are all teenagers. At first I assumed the group may have been positive, allowing the members to find support and belonging. This was indeed the case, but many posted pictures of themselves self-harming on the group page as a kind of performance sport.

Sarah is a fifteen-year-old girl who presented to see me soon after threats of expulsion were made by her high school principal. She had a degree of spunk about her, dressed in a slightly torn, maroon T-shirt with love hearts emblazoned across it. The eye contact she made was interspersed with occasional looks of scorn towards her mother. Sarah had long-term problems associated with poor impulse control, occasional self-harm and a poor sense of boundaries. This likely had something to do with her disrupted upbringing in multiple broken homes, temporary blended families and absent father figures. Her father was in and out of prison, mainly for drug-related crimes. In spite of her difficulties, it was apparent Sarah was bright and also knew how to press buttons. She would have been unaware of the controversies surrounding psychiatry and to what extent the field is based on sound medical evidence, but one of her first statements touched on the tensions between mad and bad: "What can psycho-babble and your tablets do for a bad kid. I'm a bad kid, aren't I?" she said.

Her presentation raised important issues about what constitutes group identity, especially how the online might help or complicate our sense of belonging.

Sarah had been self-harming every few months for almost two years. She remembered the first time she cut herself with a razor blade on the sensitive side of her forearm. She experienced an initial surge of pain but an associated release of frustration. She was able to hide the scars by dressing in long sleeves, even in the height of summer.

She discovered an internet forum that included other self-harmers. She was intrigued that there were others who engaged in such a behaviour, and no longer felt as isolated and alone. In an ironic twist, she felt more comfortable about self-harming. After cutting herself she jumped online and joined her macabre, self-harmer's group chat.

This progressed to posting photos of herself in the act of cutting or showing the scars of the lacerations. The online forum then exploded into photos of other members posting their own encounters, including other methods of self-harm, such as burning cigarette butts onto the skin or violent scratching. This produced a strong sense of belonging and validation for an otherwise pathological behaviour.

The group did have the aim of attempting to help its members stop the harmful behaviours, but it also helped diminish the stigma otherwise associated with the activity. This was one of the new implications of the internet, its ability to normalise otherwise pathological behaviours. Even paedophiles, terrorists and Satan worshippers had forums to help them organise and feel validated.

Sarah also posted regularly on social media, primarily Instagram and Facebook, although the latter was becoming a no-go zone given that her grandmother had an account. Her mother and other relatives did not know how to use Instagram and had not heard of Snapchat, where messages disappear within hours of being published. But Sarah had a certain exhibitionism that was not healthy in the online environment. She posted parts of her anatomy, which then led to peers at school criticising her but simultaneously sharing the photos of her topless body. This filtered back to the teachers. As a result she was facing expulsion, especially given she had previously been suspended for swearing at a teacher.

My role was to engage her, build some modicum of trust with a teenager who rarely had consistent male figures in her life and help her understand the dynamics of her distress.

Self-harm often has overlaps with what is known as borderline syndrome, a personality type that is acutely sensitive to feeling abandoned, criticised or rejected. This was even more pronounced amid the peer relations and need for group belonging that exist in adolescence. Such patients often have a history of trauma in their childhood, or a disrupted bonding with their mothers. Sarah fitted this mould. Medications could help to manage some of the complications, such as reducing anxiety, providing better impulse control and helping to regulate mood. She often complained of wildly gyrating moods, a feature of borderline personality that made sufferers think they were experiencing bipolar disorder.

There is a strong link between a chronic sense of shame and the self-harm that borderline personality sufferers endure. Shame is a self-conscious emotion closely linked to our perceptions of the opinion of others, which is especially paramount for teenagers. Females are especially affected, as a result of the magnified pressures girls face around appearance and sexuality. As someone with daughters entering their teenage years, I couldn't help worry about the challenges they face in today's world of unending novelty and associated threat.

Self-harm may also overlap with a decline of ritual in modern life. Mental health problems often arise during transition periods in our life. Initiation rites are common in facilitating the process from immaturity to maturity, especially in eyes of a relevant community. Such processes do not exist formally in Western societies. Self-harm may be an attempt to reclaim such rituals, especially given laceration or performative harm played a role in the initiation rites of traditional societies.

Sarah's case illustrates some of the dynamics surrounding shame and group identity. A key problem was her inability to form a healthy sense of connection with her peers at school. She was prone to outburst and paranoid that others thought negatively of her. At school she varied from being anxious and avoidant to disruptive and overwhelmed. But she was able to form some sense of group identity online. While this was beneficial in some respects, it also warped her sense of what constituted normal behaviour, including what may or may not be acceptable in terms of self-disclosure. Her act of posting inappropriate, sexualised photos of herself, an attempt to belong in the sphere outside her self-harmers' forum, led to her being ostracised. The confines of her room turned out to be an extension of her school playground while she was online, and all her deficiencies in appropriate interactions were magnified in that space. This is a pointer to what may be new about self-harm in our hyperconnected society, increasingly knitted together via social media. I tell parents social media is rarely the cause of mental health problems but it can magnify existing ones, such as bullying or self-harm.

This kind of shame has overlaps with the fame dynamic that theologian Andy Crouch described, especially associated with the social media-saturated world of youth.

In a wave of recent books looking at adolescents and mental health, there is agreement that the modern generation does seem to have greater difficulty managing the vicissitudes of their existence. American psychologist Jean Twenge, in a book called *IGen*, says the current crop of teenagers is woefully underprepared for the challenges of adulthood. She cites a clear correlation with the rise of smartphones. She is careful not to imply cause, but the increased incidence of mental health disorders among teens has risen sharply as smartphone use soared from 2007.

The underlying causes of self-harm are why the issue is relevant in a discussion about shame and negative emotion. The vast majority of self-harmers speak of feeling a wave of relief when they self-harm. The urge is not always conscious, which frustrates parents and loved ones who start becoming resentful. The vast majority of self-harmers speak of their sense of frustration or tension. While they are not always aware of it, many experience an overwhelming rage, usually because something they wanted was not received.

Like my patient, self-harm is often associated with what is known as borderline personality disorder, a disorder of childhood trauma that results in an intense sensitivity to feeling rejected or abandoned. Females are more likely to suffer. Many teenagers will self-harm if they don't receive an immediate response from a close friend or love interest on a messaging app. While few will admit it, the act is often an expression of rage in those who have not learned to deal with frustration. Sometimes self-harm is a way to manipulate the environment, to get what they want from those who have power, be they parents, nurses or prison wardens.

The other complicating factor about self-harm, and a clue about its origins, is that the patients show little visible emotion during interviews. They might be talking about the most horrific things, but there is barely any change in their facial expression. In my trade, we label this as a lack of reactivity in affect. Its wider significance is a roadblock between what is being experienced at an emotional level and what is expressed outwardly. This is the case in self-harm, where sufferers have adapted in the context of either abusive, conflicted, or emotionally constricted environments to repress difficult emotions like anger or aggression.

One of the key treatments for self-harm, especially for those who have a diagnosis of borderline personality disorder, is dialectical behavioural therapy (DBT). This was developed by American psychologist Marsha Linehan, who describes her treatment as a modification of cognitive behavioural therapy incorporating elements of acceptance and mindfulness inspired by Buddhist meditation. In a profile in the *New York Times*, Linehan describes suffering mental illness herself and coming to a "radical acceptance":

> One night I was kneeling in there, looking up at the cross, and the whole place became gold – and suddenly I felt something coming toward me... It was this shimmering experience, and I just ran back to my room and said, 'I love myself.' I felt transformed.

When I ask patients about the most useful concepts they learn from the DBT treatment, a regular reply is the notion of "being comfortable with the uncomfortable". When I googled this expression I found a viral TED talk by a Nigerian American blogger Luvvie Ajayi, but it is also a slogan I have heard among psychologists, especially those who work with trauma victims. Another way of thinking about the expression is the skill of handling difficult or problematic emotions, especially those associated with anger, aggression or disgust.

A key aspect of good mental health is being able to communicate distress in healthy ways. This links back to the ideas of defence mechanisms, the coping methods we use to deal with life's stressors such as humour or exercise. Self-harmers often use unhealthy coping mechanisms, such as repression, projection or avoidance. Those around them often can't tell how distressed they are, but the sufferer becomes resentful that loved ones can't read their mind.

There are many factors contributing to the current spike in psychological distress. They include the decline of communal structures, the dilution of uniting moral systems such as religion, and the greater social comparison that comes with a media-rich environment combined with a meritocratic system. But the growth in self-harm comes at a very specific time, when there has been an enormous growth in the positive psychology movement.

Positive psychology is not short of critics. Even its most charismatic leader, Martin Seligman, has redefined the movement away from what he describes as a shallow "happiology" to a greater focus on the conditions for better flourishing and the cultivation of meaning.

But examining the attraction and growth of positive psychology is important to understand the sidelining of negative emotions in recent decades, one that is closely linked to broad cultural trends.

The roots of positive psychology originate with one of the great psychological thinkers, Abraham Maslow, in the mid-twentieth century. For several decades Freud's ideas dominated the way therapists thought about their patients. There were notable challenges from thinkers like Jung, but the wider premise of primitive instincts and conflict among unconscious desires as being the key driver of psychological distress remained.

Maslow is famous for coining the notion of a hierarchy of needs, a pyramid illustrating that once we achieve our basic needs for food, shelter and sex, we aspire for higher satisfactions, such as engaging with a greater purpose, best done in activities that utilise our core skills. Maslow also outlined the importance of experiences that generated awe, something that all organised religions have understood, as evidenced by the grand edifices and rituals at the heart of all great faiths.

But an implication of Maslow's teachings was to highlight that the psychological sciences need not be just about disease and pathology; that there was a place for the uplifting and positive.

The term "positive psychology" first appeared in Maslow's publication *Motivation and Personality* in 1954 as one of the chapter titles. In it he outlines the basis for what would become a movement over the following half century:

> The science of psychology has been far more successful
> on the negative than on the positive side; it has revealed
> to us much about man's shortcomings, his illnesses, his
> sins, but little about his potentialities, his virtues, his
> achievable aspirations, or his full psychological height.
> It is as if psychology had voluntarily restricted itself to
> only half its rightful jurisdiction, and that the darker,
> meaner half.

Such a strategy reshaped psychology as attractive to a wider group of people, not least in large institutions such as business and government – the vast majority of people were not mentally unwell and may not have considered psychiatry as relevant to them.

The term self-actualisation arose out of Maslow's work and is often used today in our attempts to achieve a higher state of being. Maslow was Jewish and rebelling against what he saw as the dark forces of human nature arising from the world wars. He wondered what made people angry and hateful. He also wrote about the authoritarian mind, a field of literature that has made a big comeback in the past decade.

Another psychologist, Carl Rogers, built on Maslow's work to highlight the importance of character strengths. Rogers criticised both psychoanalysis and behaviourism as being too deterministic. He believed that for a person to achieve self-actualisation he needed an emotional environment that provided acceptance, openness and empathy. Positive psychology was seen as a way to encourage and build strengths, supplementing psychotherapy that focuses on negative emotions like sorrow and anger.

The notion of authenticity and self is linked to Rogers and Maslow, sometimes grouped in the category of a humanistic psychology.

Psychologists had in the past traditionally stayed away from questions such as character and virtue, believing they should be left to philosophers to focus on the morality of what we do. But one of the achievements of positive psychology is embracing the moral or metaphysical as fair game, to be tackled by the psychological sciences. And this is reasonable, given most people today describe their experience through the language of self-help and psychology.

The second half of the twentieth century can be seen through the prism of a more optimistic view of human nature in rebellion to the first half, which was littered with global wars and the Great Depression. The movements of self-esteem and pride helped propel some of the civil rights momentum of the 1960s and 70s. The messages of inferiority that many minority groups had absorbed were corrected.

The term "authenticity" and its application to living a more meaningful life also took shape. The idea of an authentic self can be traced back to philosopher Charles Taylor's work *The Ethics of Authenticity* from the late eighteenth century. Taylor argued that we had a moral sense and a feeling for what might be right. This feeling was, in his opinion, a link with God, a kind of moral guide.

Enlightenment thinkers, like the French philosopher Jean-Jacques Rousseau, took the notion of authenticity a step further, arguing that Man was essentially good. The Christian notion of original sin was a corruption of our true selves and limited our potential, according to Rousseau.

In his autobiography, *Confessions*, Rousseau starts with this passage:

> I have entered upon a performance which is without
> example, whose accomplishment will have no imitator.
> I mean to present my fellow immortals with a man in
> all the integrity of nature; and this man shall be myself.
> I know my heart, and have studied mankind; I am not
> made like any one I have been acquainted with, perhaps
> like no one in existence; if not better, I at least claim
> originality.

Rousseau captures the modern mantra that being yourself, something to be discovered via a degree of navel gazing, has an inherent value.

The moral worth of the individual is a critical concept. While Christianity always incorporated such a value, its upgrading during the Enlightenment allowed for the modern state, one where reason could be applied separate from God, the very heart of the West's success. But the upgrading of the importance of feelings and desire took an alternative direction.

By the 1960s, influential psychoanalysts like Rollo May wrote,

"The chief problem of people in the mid decade of the twentieth century is emptiness." May argued that people were not adequately aware of their feelings. As a result they didn't know whether their inner life was theirs or not. The path to a truly meaningful life lay in getting in better touch with one's feelings.

The growth of positive psychology can trace its origins through Rousseau, Maslow and May. The movement shifted focus away from mental illness to emotional wellbeing. Broad audiences were reached often by experts who stated the obvious but offered a scientific basis, such as studies showing that quality friendships improved our sense of psychological wellbeing. This laid the foundation for the worship of the self, sealed off from such external sources as history, nature and society. People increasingly yearn for salvation through wellbeing, health and psychic security within a climate that is more therapeutic than religious.

Much of the self-help industry is a flow-on from the original tenets of cognitive behavioural thinking, which aims to modify negative thoughts, to improve painful emotions. There has been much caricature of books such as the The Secret, which reduce the ideas to especially simplistic, almost supernatural qualities of attracting what you wish for. The world's most famous life coach, Tony Robbins, also incorporates all the elements of cognitive behavioural thinking but delivers them in a charismatic performance full of inspirational personal anecdotes.

Other earlier, important books include the blockbuster The Power of Positive Thinking, by pastor Norman Vincent Peale. Published in 1952, the book has sold twenty million copies. Typical quotes include, "change your thoughts and you can change your world", "there's only one corner of the universe that you can be sure of improving and that's your own self", and "the most common way people give up power is thinking they don't have any". A pointer to the co-opting of religious rituals is obvious in Peale's recommendation to say, "I believe", every morning.

The variety of discoveries throughout the late twentieth century helped to lay the foundations of positive psychology as we know it. But other discoveries from disciplines outside traditional psychology, such as Buddhism and pharmacology, helped shift the psychological sciences to focus beyond the unwell.

Some of the most interesting research came from Hungarian American psychologist Mihaly Csikszentmihalyi. He discovered through the practice of experience sampling, taking reports of people in a wide variety of activities at the time of their actions, that when people engaged in activities that challenged and stimulated them, they might lose awareness of time for a period. The concept became known as flow.

The more activities we can engage in that give us a sense of flow, including in leisure, as well as using our signature strengths, the more likely we are to report a sense of satisfaction about our lives. This is one of the most important and influential concepts to have come from positive psychology, one that lies at the foundation of many human resources and management philosophies in today's corporate world.

The renowned psychiatrist Viktor Frankl wrote the memoir *Man's Search for Meaning* from his experience in the Nazi concentration camps of World War II. A key concept that arose from his work is the notion of post-traumatic growth, that great adversity could be transformative and allow for deeper, more engaged existence. He coined the therapy known as logo therapy, from *logos*, the

Greek word for "meaning". The therapy has been promoted by major figures, varying from Facebook CEO Sheryl Sandberg and Australian journalist Leigh Sales in her bestseller, *Any Ordinary Day*.

Closer to my daily work, the notion of neurochemistry having a key role in positive emotions put greater pressure on physicians to supply something other than "common unhappiness". The promise of a pharmacological utopia was within reach.

While psychiatric medications were already being widely used, especially tranquillisers and anti-psychotics, neuroscientist James Old's research at McGill University in the 1950s into stimulating the brains of rats, leading them to pursue pleasure, highlighted the importance of the reward and pleasure pathways. The rats repeatedly pressed levers to receive tiny jolts of electricity delivered through implants in their brain.

While the potential of a pleasure centre in the brain offered hope for psychiatric treatments, other findings illustrated the limits of our yearnings for happiness.

An important term in the research, the notion of a "hedonic treadmill", appeared in the 1970s, drawing on adaptation level theory – how we judge an outcome depends on contrast, constancy and adaptation, influencing the perception of past and future.

The scientists who coined the term were Phillip Brickman and and Donald Campbell writing that "even as we contemplate our satisfaction with a given accomplishment, the satisfaction level fades, to be replaced finally by a new indifference and a new level of striving" prompting "men to live on a hedonic treadmill, to seek new levels of stimulation merely to maintain old levels of subjective pleasure", but never achieving any permanent happiness or satisfaction.

The hedonic treadmill became a critical foundation of happiness studies, a tributary of the wave of studies linked to positive psychology that took a different direction towards public policy.

While positive psychology's focus tended to be on the individual, happiness studies drifted further towards the political. Its theories are used to argue against measures of economic success such as GDP, as being unable to measure things beyond economic activity. Some of the most important proponents of such thinking include the world leaders Jacinda Ardern of New Zealand and Nicola Sturgeon from Scotland. Jacinda Ardern has been vocal in saying that New Zealand will incorporate a wellbeing budget with greater spending on mental health, poverty and homelessness in parallel with GDP measurements.

Happiness studies and the hedonic treadmill was taken up with gusto within branches of economics, most notably by the economist Richard Easterlin. He discovered people's happiness declined in the 1960s despite greater prosperity, which he attributed to an "escalation in human aspirations", and subsequently this paradox was named after him. While there have been studies since refuting the Easterlin paradox that subjective wellbeing is not clearly linked with GDP per capita, his work remains highly influential among anti economic growth advocates.

An American psychologist who can be considered in the pantheon of positive psychology is Ed Diener. He wrote an influential essay titled "Subjective Wellbeing" published in the journal of Personality and Social Psychology in 1984. Measured in three domains of life satisfaction, positive and negative affect, the term caught fire for its interchangeability with happiness, such that Diener was thereafter titled Dr Happiness by Time magazine.

Other important research not directly under the psychology banner but influential in the movement, included that of Paul Ekman, who studied facial expressions. Ekman discovered there was a considerable universality of facial expressions across racial and cultural boundaries. He also argued there was too much focus on negative emotions such as anger, fear and disgust, inspiring others to emphasise the transformative power of positive emotions. To some extent the notion of "fake it till you make it" has its origins in Ekman's work, because he discovered that positive facial expressions can help lead to internal positive emotions, even if the initial expression was not always spontaneous.

The triumph of many aspects of the positive psychology movement is especially highlighted by its ascendancy in popular culture. The most significant media figure of modern times, Oprah Winfrey, shifted her television program from personal problems to personal opportunities, influenced by Seligman's ideas. "I am more dedicated than ever to try and do television that inspires us to make positive changes in our lives," said Oprah.

Gratitude and kindness rituals are also secular attempts to bring in practices of prayer, as encouraged by positive psychology thinkers. They aim to thwart our tendency to adapt immediately to positive events in our lives, forever chasing the next pleasurable activity. The novel practice being taken up in Silicon Valley of dopamine fasting is along the same lines. While a fancy sounding term, it refers to depriving ourselves of activities that give bursts of pleasure varying from checking social media, sexual activity or consuming drugs. Dopamine is the chemical most associated with pleasurable events.

Billion dollar industries like executive coaching are driven by positive psychology proponents. Staff engagement policies in corporations are also modelled on theories of flow and motivation, arising from Maslow and Csikszentmihalyi.

Michelle Walder, chief executive of coaching company TXG, captures the attitudinal shift succinctly. "Coaching used to be remedial," she says. "Now it's a pragmatic tool improving performance." Motivational speakers cheer on executives while coffee mugs branded with inspirational messages remind them to keep their minds on positivity. Corporations are employing chief happiness officers or Jolly Good Fellows in the case of Google, whose mission it is to monitor positivity in the organisation. At the World Economic Forum in 2014, attendees were given a gadget to link with their bodies, which sent messages to their smartphones with feedback on their level of wellbeing. One critic after the forum wrote, "happiness as a measurable, visible, improvable entity had penetrated the citadel of global economic management".

This type of influence is significant because affluent countries are now primarily service-based economies. They place an emphasis on self-presentation and interpersonal interaction. There is a much greater importance in the modern worker presenting a cheerful, optimistic version of themselves in the public space, further limiting the space for the inevitable, difficult emotional content. This can place more pressure on our intimate relationships at home, where there can be a magnified release.

Closer to home, positive psychology has been taken up with gusto not just by the corporate sector, but by some of our most prestigious educational institutions, like Geelong and Knox Grammar schools. Geelong Grammar, for example, has on its website that its school philosophy encourages its students in "feeling and doing good". This approach may be harmless, but it is a pointer to the potential excesses that the cultural success of positive psychology might promote.

Further evidence that Australian counsellors have been especially influenced are outlined by the fact they comprised almost ten percent of the total attendees at one of the biggest conferences for positive psychology in recent history, the 2015 Fourth World Congress on Positive Psychology held in Florida. The Aussies formed the largest group of overseas attendees, despite living on the other side of the world.

The award-winning American professor of psychology, Barbara Held, has titled the dark side of the movement as "the tyranny of the positive". Held, like me, believes positivity has become too entrenched in Western institutions – we should all "think positively" to the point where some positive psychologists encourage us to inflate our self-image, be "resource oriented" and see problems as interesting "challenges". Even seriously ill people are encouraged to "learn from the illness" as part of the mantra of resilience and post-traumatic growth. Our culture has little tolerance for those who can't see the positive in the face of adversity. Nothing can be experienced negatively for its own sake. According to Held:

> The TPA (tyranny of positive attitude) has two component parts: First, you feel bad about whatever pain has come your way, then you are made to feel guilty or defective if you can't be grateful for what you do have, move forward [or] focus on the positives. This is the double punch, and it's the second part that does the most serious damage.

One outcome of the unchallenged focus on positivity is "blaming the victim" – explaining away forms of human suffering or inadequacy as being caused by the relevant individual's alleged lack of an appropriately positive or optimistic view of life. Instead Held advocates what she sees as the healthy practice of kvetching, which is Yiddish for grumbling. This is a kind of defensive pessimism.

In the same vein Danish psychologist Svend Brikmann advises in his anti-self-help book *Stand Firm* to sack your coach and go read a novel, a cultural product Brikmann argues gives much greater insights into life's rich tapestry than any life coach could possibly offer. An excess of positive thinking can become a form of denial, an excuse not to take appropriate action.

Self-help books that advertise themselves as manuals to find happiness can have a negative impact on the understanding of emotions, says Brinkmann. The underlying idea that anyone can make herself feel happy implies that unhappy people are to blame for their own misfortune.

"Mandatory happiness has become a kind of totaliarianism," says Brinkmann in an interview to online magazine *Quartz*.

In the US, mandatory happiness became the theme of an official workplace ruling against T-Mobile in May 2016, where the country's workplace mediator determined that employers cannot demand employees to be consistently upbeat.

A notable 2017 study, published in the *Journal of Personality and Social Psychology*, analysed the link between acceptance of negative emotions and mental health among 1300 adults. "We found that people who habitually accept their negative emotions experience fewer negative emotions, which adds up to better psychological health", said the study's senior author, Iris Mauss, an associate professor of psychology at UC Berkeley.

The study found that feelings of sadness, anger or disappointment inflicted more damage on people who avoided them or criticised themselves intensely for even experiencing them.

Talking to *Berkeley News* study lead author Brett Ford said, "It turns out that how we approach our own negative emotional reactions is really important for our overall well-being." The assistant professor of psychology added: "People who accept these emotions without judging or trying to change them are able to cope with their stress more successfully."

While this is just one study, I began this chapter with a description of the growth in self-harm because the confronting act is linked to an inability to tolerate negative emotions. The negative emotion is often steeped in a degree of shame. Our attitudes to shame are a forerunner to our wider stigmatisation of negative emotions, a trend that has been turbocharged in recent decades with the influence of positive psychology. This trend has limited our ability to engage healthily in groups.

Similarly, the cultural centrality of feelings and perceptions as a source of truth has harmed many people for whom feelings are the problem, built on marked misinterpretations. Much like smartphones, those most at risk from the wider cultural elevation of positivity are those who are yet to develop the psychological sophistication and flexibility that comes with maturity.

Negative emotions are critical to a healthy interaction with people and the world around us. Sadness is an appropriate response to adversity and tragedy. Guilt and shame regulate our morality and relationships to groups. It is appropriate we become angry in the face of perceived injustice. Happiness is welcome and positive, but it should not be an ubiquitous duty.

CHAPTER FOUR

Imagined Groups

The re-emergence of shame suggests it may retain a beneficial place in the health of our psyche, both individual and collective. The cultural elevation of positivity in combination with a more medicalised language for our internal experience leave primitive emotions like shame out in the cold.

A good place to consider useful roles for shame is in group therapy, an important but under-utilised aspect of mental health treatment. Shame is in many respects a proxy for group ties.

Group therapy emerged as an arm of therapeutic practice in the 1930s and 40s, initially focusing on alcoholics as well as cancer sufferers. In his seminal book on the principles of group therapy, Stanford University professor Irvin Yalom wrote that group therapy helped give support, allowed for altruism among sufferers, encouraged group cohesiveness among people who lacked such connections, and helped people gain greater self-awareness in social situations.

There are no shortages of patients who credit groups, especially those around drug addiction, as life saving. One of the original founders of Alcoholics Anonymous, Robert Smith, stated as much. A powerful aspect of group therapy is that it helps re-establish in people their nature as social beings.

Despite the modern focus on finding oneself, we largely exist in relation to other people. This awareness begins notably during adolescence, when the key task is to separate psychologically from our parents, a conflict described by Swedish psychiatrist Erik Erikson as identity versus role diffusion. The way we form our identity is through our interactions with our peer group. This is also why so many mental disorders come to light during the teenage years. Those who have problems forming relationships or completing complex tasks can often coast through primary school where the stakes tend to be lower, but their psychologically frailties tend to be exposed during high school.

A common question I ask when assessing patients is what they were like in the high school playground, a pointer to why all those American movies on the topic are so popular. The way we view ourselves in the high school playground as to being a nerd, jock or eccentric tends to play a powerful role in our self-image for life. This is particularly notable for teenagers who may have grown up in non-Western countries where social relations are not as complex, especially those where there are stricter boundaries between the sexes.

The social complexities of Western playgrounds tend to be more pronounced. This is noticeable in teenage patients of mine newly arrived from either Asia or the Middle East who find the looser boundaries regarding sexuality and interactions between the genders both alluring but challenging. The potential for humiliating rejection seems much greater.

Many people with mental illness often have a poor awareness of how other people view them. This can have its upside. Some of the people we euphemistically label as having personality disorders can be intolerable or irritating, yet they are blissfully unaware of the effect they have on others. This can come to a head in later life, however, after an especially tolerant partner gives up on them or they keep losing employment.

When I was taught interviewing techniques, I learnt that when there are physically two people in a room, it's worth conceptualising the interaction as between multiple others. There is the you as you perceive yourself, as you really are, and as how the other person views you. And vice versa.

What is more common are the thousands of people who are cut off from healthier relationships because they are terrified at the prospect of negative scrutiny. This is what I wrote in a previous chapter, about those people who are especially sensitive to negative self-evaluation at the expense of receiving any signals towards affiliation.

One of the most satisfying aspects of group therapy is in helping such shy avoiders re-orient themselves towards affiliation. The challenge is usually getting them to attend. I have had patients who hid in their vehicles in the car park for the length of the session but, with further encouragement, were eventually able to attend. Group therapy is especially important for those with some version of social anxiety, which is often grounded in elements of shame.

This subject of shame is rarely discussed in group therapy, probably because of stigma. Multiple studies have shown that dieting works much better if it's connected to some kind of group, such as Weight Watchers. This is partly about accountability – having someone to face and measure your actual application, or lack thereof, when it comes to diet and exercise. But shame's power lies in group cohesiveness. When a group becomes cohesive and the members feel a genuine stake in the other members' welfare, that's when the magic really takes effect.

While it is rarely called as such, this is the nature of a more reintegrative shaming. When members of an addiction group are able to admit to failings in staying abstinent there may be a brief shaking of heads from other members or a pause to acknowledge the important information. For the act to be useful, the confessing member must feel a small amount of shame in letting other members of the group down, but there is an immediate signal from the others along the lines of encouragement and getting themselves back on track.

If a patient feels too embarrassed or humiliated they may not attend. Alternatively they merely become defensive and blame others. But if they have not formed any bonds at all, they won't feel any shame. My experience in journalism is an example of transgressing a group's boundaries in part because I was not terribly well integrated into the group's norms and values.

The power of group therapy in helping people heal is a great example of shame's usefulness. This depends upon the reintegrative aspect of the emotion being ingrained, an automatic expectation.

When discussing the world of social media, religious leaders have raised the prospect that without the concept of sin, our society lacks the structure to allow for forgiveness. The alternative is ostracism and exile without a route for reunion. Even groups such as those for weight loss or drug addiction contain aspects that incorporate Christian concepts of forgiveness.

Martin Luther King spoke about forgiveness being an attitude rather than an act. In group therapy a space is created where people can confess to their secular "sins" of using drugs or consuming high calorie foods. There is then the prospect of accountability, some encouragement towards directive treatment and finally an act of reconciliation towards trusting the member again. Community solidarity is strengthened by the entire process.

While Western societies are predicated on the idea of the individual, we underestimate our connection to groups. While we are mostly like apes, we are also a bit like bees.

The American political theorist Francis Fukuyama writes in his book *Identity* that one of the weaknesses of liberal democracy is that it does not prioritise the importance of group identity. The system does not easily incorporate groups into the political framework. This lack of a strong collective identity leaves room for identity politics to emerge. Furthermore, the system gives little direction into what might constitute the good life or the deeper conditions for human flourishing other than individual freedoms constrained by limitations on harm to others.

But we forget that our experiment with the individual at the heart of a civic state is barely a few hundred years old. For the vast bulk of human history, we have existed in tribes, usually not larger than fifty or sixty in total. The American journalist Sebastian Junger, in his book *Tribe*, outlines this number as the largest group still able to be marshalled effectively within a hierarchy and leadership. Army battalions rarely go beyond such a number. Nor do corporate teams answering to a particular manager. In the online world this picture becomes more complicated, as such numerical boundaries blur.

When thinking about the nature of groups in our internet mediated world, a relevant concept is the notion of an imagined group. The term originated from a paper about nationalism written by Irish political scientist Benedict Anderson. He argued that nations depended upon our ties to an imagined community, given we didn't know the vast bulk of other citizens:

> [The nation] is imagined as a community, because, regardless of the actual inequality and exploitation that may prevail in each, the nation is always conceived as a deep, horizontal comradeship. It is this fraternity that makes it possible, over the past two centuries, for so many millions of people, not so much to kill, as willingly to die for such limited imaginings.

Anderson cites the common language that media like newspapers create within countries as critical in forming such an arrangement, a trend less likely at a time of media fragmentation.

Imagined community is not a mental health concept and nor am I a sociologist. I am usually assessing patients individually. But imagined groups strike a chord as to how so many patients are trapped in their minds, fretting and avoiding some notion of the group that they would both like to be a part of but are also terrified of rejection. The fear relates back to one of the theories of social anxiety – that such individuals are attuned to cues and signs of dominance at the expense of attunement to signals of affiliation. They avoid undertaking actions that might be seen as trying to compete for approval or status within their notion of an imagined group. Their mental habits have predisposed them to anticipating negative scrutiny. This is a trait of living in the privatised, urban suburbia.

A good example of imagined groups is when we think of the problem of terrorism, especially the lone wolf variety. I have had the opportunity to assess such cases for psychiatric evaluations and have grown up in an Islamic community where discussions about the topic are impossible to escape.

Whether it be the white nationalist or Islamic jihadist variety, both types depend upon an attachment built through online interactions. The virtual community of believers is perceived to be under threat, via infidel Christian Westerners to the Islamic fundamentalist, or by Muslims to the hardened white nationalist. They are in some respect Newtonian reactions, in that the reaction is an equal and opposite one.

The killer in the Christchurch massacre, Brenton Tarrant, visited the sites of many battles throughout the Balkans and other parts of Europe that he interpreted as great Christian victories over Mohammedan invaders. Even the Bulgarian foreign minister, Ekaterina Zakharieva, was flummoxed at such an intensity of interest about her country and region. "A very serious knowledge of the Balkan history in details I would say even few people in the Balkans know," she told Reuters, when asked about Tarrant's travels.

The vast majority of lone wolf Islamist attacks have included individuals who formed some kind of online identity despite few physical interactions with those of tribal affiliation. This is especially true as anti-terrorism strategies, intense security and intelligence operations have had success at limiting two-way interactions between individuals or among groups.

While I recognise terrorism is an extreme example, I see similarities in many of my patients who exist a great deal within imagined communities when forming identities.

This may include the playground among adolescent patients unable to attend school. The imagined group may consist of former friends from school or work among patients struggling to leave their households, distant colleagues only visible on social media for patients on compensation claims unable to return to work, or just ill-defined but prospective groups of people ready to make negative judgements.

This is where the concept of shame is so closely linked to social anxiety and ultimately to one of the great afflictions limiting human flourishing today – the lack of affiliations. There have been multiple studies outlining the fall in our group connections, from the lack of church attendance to the dramatic decline in memberships of unions or political parties. Seminal books such as *Bowling Alone* by Harvard academic Robert Putnam and *Coming Apart* by Charles Murray have statistically outlined our fractured selves.

A quote from Putnam's book captures a key problem that I see in my work as contributing to mental health problems:

> For the first two-thirds of the twentieth century a pow-
> erful tide bore Americans into ever deeper engagement
> in the life of their communities, but a few decades ago
> – silently, without warning – that tide reversed and we
> were overtaken by a treacherous rip current. Without
> at first noticing, we have been pulled apart from one
> another and from our communities over the last third
> of the century.

Australia may be partially protected by our sheer, relative pros-
perity, but the trends are playing out throughout the Western world. As someone who sees individuals' emotional distress, but has also had involvement in a range of community groups, I see something of a contradiction in a whole range of people seeking group ties

and better relationships in parallel with a host of organisations finding it increasingly difficult to attract volunteers.

Much of this is due to the frenetic pace of life, where both parents are working and attempting to raise children. The urban sprawl and the anonymity of suburbia are also contributing factors. In his book, Putnam quotes the American journalist Walter Lippmann: "[W]e have changed our environment more quickly than we know how to change ourselves".

While Putnam proposes a host of state interventions, such as greater employer support of community programs, my interest is in what might be holding us back psychologically. Humans have the complex ability of being able to imagine how we are perceived in the minds of others. This is heightened even further in the age of technology where the mental landscape is enervating and confusing. Our minds are forever rubbing up against other minds, even while we're physically alone. While tightly knit groups always encouraged conformity and self-conscious behaviour, our disconnected, modern societies still require the exhaustion of thinking while considering what other people might be thinking about our thoughts.

The notion of being "other directed" was first coined by American scholar David Riesman in his bestselling book *The Lonely Crowd*. Riesman argued that the nineteenth century in the West encouraged people to be more inner directed, in what he termed as a "gyroscope". Our behaviour was internalised at an early age from our parents and elders. While our early life remains paramount, our behaviour today is more a like a radar monitoring the peer group and the media. The peer group can also be construed increasingly either online or imagined.

Riesman's prescient observation was the loss of clear-cut boundaries between the public and private, with leisure and work, or between audiences and performers. There was a greater slipperiness in life. In parallel with this slipperiness, society had shifted from one based on scarcity and production to one where consumption was a social act. This presaged the term "post-industrial" in reference to white collar activities being linked to sales, service and consumption. The skills valued today are exactly what Riesman implied by the term "other directed". The modern workplace values those that are skilled at horizontal communication and not those obeying orders and dishing them out in a rigid hierarchy.

This has possibly changed a step further today to attitudes trumping consumption, the origin of the much derided but utilised term "virtue signalling". The value of consumption as a marker of status has been diluted as outsourced mass production has made things cheaper, but enlightened views on charged political topics may now rank as a conspicuous social signal instead.

In the case of shame and social anxiety, the trend of us being other directed is contributing to a personal overestimation of the potential for ostracism and the loss of social rank. Our inability to name and discuss shame without stigma is preventing us from better grasping the opportunities for affiliation.

Just as what happens with children is sometimes referred to as canaries in the mine, self-harm and its tragic growth among adolescents is a pointer to our greater difficulty in handling negative emotions. Even the rise of figures like Trump, a kind of primitive Id of Western civilisation, is a version of the suppression of negative emotions in public form, that of political correctness.

The past half-century has seen a steady diminution in the

importance of our primitive selves and the unconscious as the promise of brain science and positivity have taken hold. A better identification and a stronger ability to signal negativity beyond its stigmatisation may be a helpful step in offering a richer tapestry and language to communicate our inner experience.

Our present moment can be seen as something of a pause to a half-century of unbridled liberalism, both social and economic, where there has been an unmooring of groups in favour of the unleashing of desires and aspirations, of expressive individualism. This can be witnessed externally through political trends of greater protectionism in trade or a stronger focus on borders in Western countries.

But there is also a parallel internal component. The rise of shame in countries that believed it had been banished is a pointer to a greater yearning for group identity when the meta-narratives of nationalism and religion are no longer apparent, at least not with the same prestige or strength. A key to helping us to form better bonds and relationships is to harness and tame one of our earliest emotions, positioned at the heart of our origin story – that of shame.

AFTERWORD

It is reassuring that even in unusual times, some things never change, such as the likelihood of a Rugby League scandal. In the midst of coronavirus restrictions, instead of any transgression involving sex or violence, the scandal comprised of a social distancing faux pas.

The incumbent NSW half back Nathan Cleary was discovered waving his arms up and down in the vicinity of several scantily clad young women recording a video to the Tik Tok social media platform. Fellow league players Latrell Mitchell, Ado-Carr and Roberts-David were also present. All received fines and brief suspensions for their prohibited getaway to a rural property against official recommendations.

While on the receiving end of pointed condemnations from the Chairman of the sport's ruling body, Peter Vlandys, and the Premier of the New South Wales, Gladys Berejiklian, a front page picture in Sydney's *Daily Telegraph* of the players with the title "Covidiots" was especially notable.

The term #Covidiot emerged online first as a hashtag. It has since been used thousands of times to criticise behaviour deemed errant, a marker of the rise of pandemic shaming.

Since the pandemic the term has been used to expose drunk spring breakers flouting advice in America to those attending a large, Stereophonic concert in Manchester. Flower markets have been pictured on twitter leading to online vitriol directed at florists accused of spreading infection risk. Public officials have been forced to resign after not living up to their own advice, including the Chief Medical Officer of Scotland and a Minister exposed holidaying at his beach house in Australia.

Shame's comeback is also being accelerated within this framework. While sidelined critics might argue the word tyranny could replace the restrictions imposed by public health authorities, in the current moment the priorities of such officials hold sway. Suddenly the acts of social distancing and appropriate hygiene have fallen into the realm of public law and order. Police prosecute those walking too closely or in excessively large groups. The act of targeted coughing is now a form of assault. Families throwing frisbees in parks have been shamed, leading to new criticism of police officials being heavy-handed. In Sydney, a man was fined for eating a kebab on a park bench alone after completing a several kilometre jog.

From drones patrolling and exposing people in Europe daring to travel outside to red flags being flown in apartment blocks where coronavirus has been identified, shame's usefulness in codifying appropriate behaviour has become paramount.

Shame is effectively a proxy for group ties and a shared morality. Its diffuse re-emergence in recent decades was a function of political tribalism reinforced by online information flows. The Left focused on those who transgressed boundaries of political correctness whereas the Right preferred targets like welfare fraud. Public health advocates had a greater tolerance for fat shaming and ostracising smokers. Meanwhile shaming associated with sexuality became increasingly rare.

But discussions around shame also indicate a yearning for a moral language stripped bare from the decline of religion. We remain morally inarticulate while existential despair has been poached by the more medicalised language of mental health.

Nothing compares with staring bald-faced at our mortality when it comes to raising moral and philosophical issues. Epidemics have changed the course of history by reshaping our worlds, both physical and existential.

Daniel Defoe wrote of the Bubonic plague in *A Journal of a Plague Year* in 1722:

> [E]very One had Death, as it were, at his Door,… the Children ran away from their parents, as they languished in the utmost distress: And in some Places…Parents did the like to their Children. for the Danger of immediate Death to ourselves, took away Bonds of Love, all Concern for one another.

From a mental health point of view, there is an added urgency, being in the background of both the health and economic crises we face.

There are aspects of mental health that fall into the non-essential category, the so-called worried well. Australia has been one of the wealthiest countries in the world having not had a recession for almost three decades, yet we still have the second highest rate of anti-depressant prescription after Iceland. The coronavirus has acted to prick a moment in Western civilisation which Israeli historian Yuval Harari calls a combination of incredible prosperity combined with a lack of purpose.

Whereas large chunks of the mental health sector oversaw neuroses of people overestimating risk, the same group are no longer as unrealistic about the potential threats on offer. Many of my patients with anxiety disorders have not deteriorated. Their distress is no longer individualised but now shared. The socially anxious are also spared the performative strains of modern life, from work meetings to the scrutiny of chance encounters.

Just as coronavirus exposes all the different fault lines and weaknesses of each society it invisibly penetrates, it has functioned as something of an exclamation mark upon a half century of social and economic liberalism. If Brexit and Trump were initial portents, an epidemic that has stymied individual autonomy has potentially slammed a historical door. Covid-19 in its uncaring destruction has further highlighted Douglas Murray's lament about modern liberalism and "the feeling that the story has run out".

The language of individual rights is being smashed by the priorities of public health, which is dependent upon mutual obligation. Just as many national insurance programs received momentum after the Spanish flu, the emotional disconnection and dilution of group ties preceding the crisis may receive a much needed tonic. The values of introspection, family, community and renewed faith are likely to gain traction.

Within this context of a more united resistance against a collective threat, the usefulness of a gentle shame is being highlighted. This is especially true in a multicultural society where a focus on individualism and self-esteem will not translate for many ethnic groups.

According to anthropologist David Jordan, shame in Chinese cultures "is the ability to take delight in the performance of one's duty." Given Chinese and Indians dominate new migrants over the past decade, the stigmatisation of shame has implications for education and the law. For example, domestic violence in ethnic communities has considerable overlaps with maintaining perceived honour, whereas alcohol and social disadvantage are stronger correlates in other demographics.

But recent outbreaks of pandemic shaming also expose the limitations. There is a tension between appropriate enforcement of acceptable behaviours to the trashing of individual dignity with no paths to forgiveness. This has been especially pronounced in the past decade through online shaming, where a host of figures both prominent and otherwise, have been deleted or cancelled due to some kind of inappropriate comment or action.

In her book *Is Shame Necessary* environmental scientist Jennifer Jacquet argues shame's ability to scale can be significant when behaviours are unacceptable, but still within the law, especially when it comes to corporations or governments which are not capable of feeling guilt:

> Digital technologies have at once lowered the cost
> of gossip and exposure and expanded gossip's speed
> and scope. This could make shame more salient to
> public life than ever before, especially since the
> power to use it has been put increasingly into the
> hands of citizens.

Jacquet cites the improvements in working conditions fashion companies were forced to undertake after global outcry when Dickensian, slave-like conditions were exposed through online shaming.

Western societies have to some extent underplayed the role of shame, deeming it negative and primitive. We are ashamed of shame.

The role of guilt has instead been elevated, seen as a morally superior emotion to regulate transgression. Shame is portrayed as the inner demon responsible for a range of psychopathology.

In their academic research about the difference between shame and guilt American psychologists Tangney and Dearing give the predominant view in our culture:

> Our lives as individuals, as social beings, and as a society can be enhanced by transforming painful, problematic feelings of shame into more adaptive feelings of guilt. Recognizing the distinction between shame and guilt is an important first step in making ours a more moral society.

Yet poorly understood shame is an unnamed undercurrent that leads people to avoidance and isolation. The emotion hides in plain sight while we pretend we have superseded it. As Salman Rushdie writes: "Dear Reader, shame is not the exclusive property of the East."

What we often call social anxiety is steeped in shame, but one coloured by perceived failures in our media rich meritocracy that breeds inadequacy. In the language of evolutionary psychology, we live an environment that encourages too many of us into acts of social submission instead of grasping towards invitations of affiliation. Symptoms of emotional distress are often signals with regards to our perceived status within groups and hierarchies, many of which are now imagined online.

Group therapy is an area of psychology which outlines the potential benefits of harnessing shame effectively. When members of an addiction group are able to admit to failings in staying abstinent there may be a brief shaking of heads from other members or a pause to acknowledge the important information. For the act to be useful, the confessing member must feel a small amount of shame in letting members of the group down, but there is an immediate signal along the lines of encouragement and getting themselves back on track.

If a patient feels too embarrassed or humiliated they may not attend. Alternatively they merely become defensive and blame others. But if they don't feel they have formed any bonds at all, they won't feel any shame. Shame implies an audience.

The power of group therapy in helping people heal is a great example of shame's usefulness, as a proxy for group identity and cohesiveness. This depends upon the reintegrative aspect of the emotion being ingrained, an automatic expectation.

When discussing the world of social media in particular, religious leaders have raised the prospect that without the concept of sin, our society lacks the structure to allow for forgiveness. The alternative is ostracism and exile without a route for reunion. Even groups such as those for weight loss or drug addiction contain aspects that incorporate Christian concepts of forgiveness.

Our current circumstances are challenging us to renew our inner lives, just as we strive to avoid the threat to our physical bodies. The rise in the discussion of mental health in recent decades corresponds with a decline in a moral, metaphysical language.

Pandemic shaming is likely to be limited to this period whereby coronavirus is the dominant force shaping our lives. But its limited re-emergence is a pointer that shame has never really left, but just lurked with alternative names or iterations.

A better understanding of shame and a focus on its reintegrative potential offer promise to enliven our emotional selves.

In the wake of a shared threat to our species, we are bonded together in a mutual dread, imagining the implications for a better future. It is time for a kind of aggressive friendship to satisfy our longing for a richer collective, a lurch to greater affiliation.

REFERENCES

Anderson, Benedict, *Imagined Communities: Reflections on the Origin and Spread of Nationalism*, Verso, 1983.

Benedict, Ruth, *The Chrysanthemum and the Sword*, Houghton Miffler Harcourt, 1946.

Brickman, P. & Campbell, D. T., "Hedonic Relativism and Planning the Good Society", In M.H. Appley (Ed.), *Adaptation-level Theory* (pp. 287-305), Academic Press 1971.

Brinkmann, Svend, "Stand Firm: Resisting the Self Improvement Craze", *Polity*, 2017.

Brown, Brene, *Listening to Shame*, TED talks, 2010.

Carey, Benedict, "Expert on Mental Illness Reveals Her Own Struggle", *New York Times*, 13 June 2011.

Chaney, Sarah, *Psyche on the Skin: A History of Self Harm*, Reaktion Books, 2017.

Crouch, Andy, "The Return of Shame", *Christianity Today*, Vol. 59, No. 2, March 2015, p. 32.

Csikszentmihalyi, M., *Flow: The Psychology of Optimal Experience*, Harper and Row (New York), 1990.

De Boitton, Alain, *Status Anxiety*, Hamish Hamilton, 2004.

Defoe, Daniel, *A Journal of the Plague Year*, Dover Publications, Republished 2001 (Original 1722).

Diamond, Jared, "The Daily Shower Can Be A Killer", *New York Times*, 28 January 2013.

Diener, E., "Subjective Wellbeing", *Psychological Bulletin*, 95, 542–575, 1984.

Easterlin, R., "Does Economic Growth Improve the Human Lot?", In P. A. David & M. W. Reder (Eds.), *Nations and Households in Economic Growth: Essays in Honour of Moses Abramovitz*, Academic Press, 1974.

Ekman, P. & Friesen, W. V., "Constants Across Cultures in the Face and Emotion", *Journal of Personality and Social Psychology*, 17(2), 124-129, 1971.

Ford, Brett, Phoebe Lam, Oliver John, Iris Mauss, "The Psychological Health Benefits of Accepting Negative Emotions and Thoughts: Laboratory, Diary, and Longitudinal Evidence", *Journal of Personality and Social Psychology*, 115(6):1075-1092, December 2018.

Frankl, Victor, *Man's Search for Meaning*, Verlag für Jugend und Volk (Austria), Beacon Press (English), 1946.

Fromm, Erich, *Man for Himself: An Inquiry into the Psychology of Ethics*, Holt Paperbacks, 1990.

Fukuyama, Francis, *Identity: The Demand for Dignity and the Politics of Resentment*, Farrar, Straus and Giroux, 2018.

Furedi, Frank, *Culture of Fear*, Bloomsbury, 1997.

Goldhill, Olivia, "'Positive Thinking has Turned Happiness into a Duty and a Burden', Says a Danish psychologist", *Quartz*, 4 March 2017.

Hazard, Paul Alfred, "Freud's Teaching on Shame", *Laval théologique et philosophique*, Vol. 25, No. 2, 1969, 234–267.

Hartenberg, Paul, *Les Timides et la Timidité*, University of California Libraries, 1910.

Herman, Judith, *Trauma and Recovery*, Ingram Publishers, 1992.

Herzberg, David, *Happy Pills in America: From Miltown to Prozac*, Johns Hopkins University Press, 2009.

Hornor, Gail, "Non Suicidal Self Injury", *Journal of Paediatric Health Care*, 1 May 2016.

Horowitz, Daniel, *Happier? The History of a Cultural Movement that Aspired to Transform America*, Oxford University Press, 2018.

Jacobs, Emma, "New Year. New You. The boom in executive coaching", *Australian Financial Review*, 6 January 2020.

Jacquet, Jennifer, *Is Shame Necessary?*, Penguin Books, 2015.

Junger, Sebastian, *Tribe: On Homecoming and Belonging*, Twelve, 2018.

Kaufman, Gersten, *Shame: The Power of Caring*, Shenkman Books, 1992.

Kaufman, Gersten, *The Psychology of Shame*, Springer, 1989.

Kaye, Byron, "In New Zealand, a Journey around the World and into Darkness", *Reuters*, 17 March 2019.

Kramer, Peter, *Listening to Prozac*, Penguin Books, 1993.

Liebowitz, Michael, "Social Anxiety Scale, Social Phobia", *Modern Problems of Pharmacopsychiatry*, 22:141-173, 1987.

Maslow, Abraham, *Motivation and Personality*, Harper and Row (New York), 1970.

May, Rollo, *The Meaning of Anxiety*, W.W. Norton and Company, 1950.

Mishra, Pankaj, *The Age of Anger*, Penguin Books, 2018.

Murray, Charles, *Coming Apart: The State of White America*, Crown, 2013.

Nasrin, Taslima, *Lajja* (shame), Penguin Books, 1993.

Olds, James, "Reward from Brain Stimulation in the Rat", *Science*, 122:878, 1955.

Peale, Norman Vincent, *The Power of Positive Thinking*, Touchstone Books, 1950.

Pinker, Steven, *The Better Angels Of Our Nature: Why Violence Has Declined*, Penguin Books, 2012.

Putnam, Robert, *Bowling Alone: The Collapse and Revival of American Community*, Touchstone Books, 2001.

Riesman, David, *The Lonely Crowd: A Study of the Changing American Character*, Yale University Press, 1960.

Routledge, Clay, *Supernatural: Death, Meaning and the Power of the Invisible World*, Oxford University Press USA, 2018.

Ronson, John, *So You've Been Publicly Shamed*, Pan Macmillan/Riverhead Press, 2015.

Rousseau, Jean Jacques, *The Confessions*, Penguin Random House, 1953 (1782).

Shatzkin, Kate, "Judges are Resorting to Shame in Sentencing Criminals", *Los Angeles Times*, 26 April 1998.

Stassel, Scott, *My Age of Anxiety*, Knopf Books, 2014.

Stearns, Peter N., *Shame: A Brief History* (History of Emotions Series), University of Illinois Press, 2017.

Tait, Amelia, "Pandemic Shaming: Is it helping us keep our distance?", *Guardian*, 5 April 2020.

Tangney, J. P., & Dearing, R. L., *Emotions and Social Behaviour: Shame and Guilt*, Guilford Press, 2002.

Taylor, Charles, *The Ethics of Authenticity*, Harvard University Press, 2018.

Twenge, Jean, *IGen: Why Today's Super-Connected Kids Are Growing Up Less Rebellious, More Tolerant, Less Happy – and Completely Unprepared for Adulthood – and What That Means for the Rest of Us*, Atria Books, 2017.